To Aunt Dorothy —
from Lloyd and Joanne
with love!

The
STREET
ADOPTER'S
HANDBOOK

Change the spiritual climate in your city . . .
one street at a time

by

Lloyd and Joanne Turner

"After this the Lord appointed seventy-two others
and sent them two by two ahead of him to every
town and place where he was about to go."

—Luke 10:1, New International Version

Printed in the United States of America

Published by Transformational Publications
A Division of Harvest Evangelism, Inc.
PO Box 20310, San Jose CA 95160-0310
Tel. 408-927-9052

www.transformourworld.org

Acknowledgments
Cover Design: Steve Martin
Document Review: Dave Thompson and Ted Hahs

I remember the phone call in 2007. A gangland-style murder had just happened in Newark, Mayor Booker was calling for the Church to "help kick the devil out of the city," and Lloyd and Joanne found themselves "ambushed by God" with an unavoidable burden to do something about it. What started that November with a very simple prayer meeting produced a prayer initiative that has adopted every street in the city, helped the city turn a corner, and produced similar initiatives in over 300 cities around the world. As members of the International Transformation Network, the Turners build off the timeless paradigms for transformation and the powerful principles of prayer evangelism defined by Ed Silvoso to give you a powerful tool to fill your city with sustainable prayer that can change it forever. The **Street Adopter's Handbook** is a must item for your transformation tool box.

Dave Thompson
Senior Vice President
Harvest Evangelism, Inc.

As you walk through these pages, your heart will be moved to see the 350-year old destiny of a city now being fulfilled. At the end of the book, you will know that you have been thoroughly equipped to take concrete steps in the streets of your community and to re- awaken the destiny of your city, your life (the Great Commission), and the Bride of Christ. Just say, "YES LORD!"

Gail Okuley
New Beginnings Fellowship, Allentown, PA
Coordinator, Pray for the Lehigh Valley

Having had the privilege of meeting and praying with Lloyd and Joanne Turner, one comes to understand the depth of their commitment and heart to see God transform not only their own city but also the cities of the world. Their book, *The Street Adopter's Handbook*, reflects their personal journey of trial and discovery. The many chapters of this book give the reader guidelines on how to launch, pray through and create momentum in keeping with the Holy Spirit. What is so appreciated is their transparency in sharing what would come to them during prayer, how they needed a prayer covering, their understanding of the importance of captains and the revelation from scriptures which cemented their efforts. When one sees what God has done in Newark, New Jersey—with ordinary people committed to pray for their streets, schools, neighbours and leaders—how can the reader not be encouraged to follow the tested wisdom found in this handbook written by those who have run the race with both humility and excellence?

Linda Ferrante

Director, Global Day of Prayer Toronto
Mission Greater Toronto Area Prayer Initiatives

This handbook is a clearly written guide to adopting streets and how to have a townwide impact by joining with other Christians to adopt every street in your town. It is very informative, and the testimonies from various towns in America and other countries in the world are most inspiring. This book tells you why you should adopt streets in prayer and also how to do this. After reading the book, it's time to put it into action and have your own testimony!

Wendy Thomas

National Prayer Coordinator
Street Pastors and School Pastors, UK

In 2009 I adopted Bryant Street (for obvious reasons!) to pray for it as my part in *Pray For Newark*. We join with hundreds of cities implementing the amazing *Adopt-A-Street Initiative,* launched by my dear friends, Lloyd and Joanne Turner. An expression of Luke 10:1 ("Jesus sent them out two by two ahead of him to every town and place where he was about to go"), this concerted prayer thrust by local churches holds great hope for cities and communities everywhere. Having served the global prayer movement for nearly 30 years, I believe this is one of the most strategic grassroots prayer outreaches anywhere today. Now the Turners place in our hands much of what the Spirit has taught them since forming the effort in 2007. Let *The Street Adopter's Handbook* equip you and your church to fulfill Luke 10—to go before the reigning Christ as you prepare by prayer for a greater manifestation of His saving Kingdom on the streets where you live.

David Bryant
President, Proclaim Hope!
Author, Christ is ALL!

What has taken place and is growing out of Newark is indeed faith activating and highly inspirational. Transformation of this urban city is well on its way and is becoming a testimony that is releasing many to follow. Understanding and tapping into the spiritual heritage and working with re-discovered, practical Biblical strategies is exactly what we need here on the old continent. Thanks to the Turners for going before us and for placing *The Street Adopter's Handbook* and tools in our hands. The rock that has been cut out—not by human hands—is now growing to become a mountain (Daniel 2:34-35).

Aarne Nurmio
Market Place Minister
President Convocatum Ltd
Espoo / Kauniainen, Finland

Contents

Preface

Today there are more than 250 Adopt-Your-Street initiatives in the U.S. and a growing number in 35+ nations around the world. Christian leaders from every continent have seen the power of God at work as they apply Prayer Evangelism principles at the street level. Some of these cities—including Newark, Flint, Jacksonville, San Antonio, and Washington, D.C.—have had problems with crime, poverty, education, housing, and other serious social issues for decades and are working with marketplace Christians to find answers to problems that appear to have no solution from a "rational" perspective.

Other cities in the Adopt-Your-Street movement—including Hilo, HI; Bethlehem, Pa; Lancaster, PA; St. Augustine, FL; and Toronto, CN—were centers of renewal in past spiritual awakenings and are eagerly preparing for the next great move of God in our nation and around the world.

The leadership team of PrayForNewark is humbled to see how prayer initiative leaders from six continents have taken our initial Adopt a Street model and applied it with great energy and creativity in their own communities. In 2007, when we launched PrayForNewark, we had a strong sense that the Lord wanted to see every street in Newark, New Jersey, prayed for on a daily basis, and so we pressed on until all 900 streets were adopted by name. During this two-year process, the Lord was gracious to provide early signs of favor, demonstrating to us that this project was near and dear to His heart.

The purpose of this **Handbook** is to summarize the principles and strategies that have proven to be effective in Adopt-Your-Street projects around the world. Regardless of what your city's felt need is today, we believe these principles, methods, and testimonies will help you to "see what you've never seen before" by "doing what you've never done before." Let the Holy Spirit guide you along the awesome "highway of holiness" that is before you. The streets, homes, schools, and businesses in the U.S. and abroad are ripe for harvest—but the workers are indeed few. Be confident that your current "day of small beginnings" is an important first step in preparing for Jesus to visit your city, and that His desire is to see your city transformed—one street at a time.

This first edition of the **Handbook** is dedicated to the believers in Newark who eagerly desire to see their city become "as nearly as possible a kingdom of God on earth," and to those who are coming to Newark to attend Harvest Evangelism's North America Conference on City Transformation on July 7-9, 2011. We welcome you as you come to experience and pray for the transformation of America's third oldest city.

In His service,

Lloyd and Joanne Turner

New Providence, New Jersey
July 2011

PART ONE

LAUNCHING YOUR INITIATIVE

CHAPTER ONE

Jesus Wants to Visit Your City

Summary: *We know that Jesus would like every person on earth to receive Him as Lord and Savior. For some inexplicable reason He has chosen to use human beings as instruments to achieve His purposes, and He instructs us to labor in fields that are ripe for harvest. The strategy He gave us to reach our cities is contained in Luke 10 and is referred to today as "Prayer Evangelism". In this **Handbook** we describe how Street Adoption is a method of implementing Prayer Evangelism that can accelerate the process of transformation in your city.*

Two of Jesus' favorite words are "come" and "go". At the beginning of His public ministry He taught the disciples to pray, "Thy kingdom come, Thy will be done." In the Sermon on the Mount, He told the people, "Come to me, all you who are heavy laden, and I will give you rest." (Matthew 11:28). He welcomed anyone who desired to come to Him (Luke 9:23), and He made a special point of inviting children to come into His presence (Matthew 19:14).

As His ministry progressed, the emphasis changed from "come" to "go". In Luke Chapter 9 he told several would-be disciples to "go and preach the kingdom of God." (9:60). In Luke 10 He commissioned seventy-two others to visit every town and place where He was about to go. And His last recorded instructions in Matthew's Gospel were, *"Go and make disciples of all the nations, baptizing them in the name of the Father and of the Son and of the Holy Spirit."* (28:18)

Despite the high standard of living found in America today, millions of people in this nation are struggling with poverty, unemployment, and hopelessness. Although our cities are filled with churches, many congregations have concentrated on "coming" in rather than "going" out to where hurting people live in our cities and rural areas. All too often, we have concentrated on getting people to "come" into our church buildings rather than sending out teams to "go" into the marketplace—which includes the business, education, and government sectors. In many urban centers today, we may see three to five churches on the same city block, but with little impact on the surrounding neighborhood. *In short, we have become focused on "coming" rather than "going".*

In Luke 10:1-9 Jesus spoke to an assembly of the seventy-two unnamed disciples and charged them to prepare the way for Him to visit the cities and places surrounding Jerusalem. He gave them specific instructions on how to prepare for the journey, how to minister to those they would meet, and what to tell them about the kingdom of God. But there is no indication that He gave them roadmaps or detailed instructions about which houses or neighborhoods to visit. These seventy-two were clearly sent out on a mission assignment— to prepare the way for Him to visit towns and places throughout the region. But the details and strategies were left to each individual. And so it is today as we implement Prayer Evangelism. We cooperate with Jesus and are led by the Holy Spirit, but we must ultimately decide which places and individuals to visit each day.

When we began the Newark Adopt-a-Street initiative in 2007, we had a strong sense that Jesus wanted to see every street in the city adopted for daily prayer. There was no master strategy or deep theological understanding on why He wanted us to adopt streets, but the PrayForNewark team had a clear conviction that Jesus wanted us to prepare every street in the city for His visitation. As we prayed about this matter and journaled the responses we heard, the Lord began to download ideas and instructions to different members of our team. One person meditated upon Isaiah 62:10 and 12, which state, *"Build up, build up the highway! . . . And you will be called Sought After, the City No Longer Deserted."* We sensed that this biblical promise to Jerusalem applies today to Newark—and to countless other cities around the world. Another team member wrote down this instruction, "As you adopt the city and people adopt streets, businesses, homes and apartment buildings, the spirit of abandonment—the orphan spirit—will be replaced by the spirit of adoption, and the spirit of bondage/slavery will be replaced by the spirit of sonship." A third member of our team had a vision of a map of our city. Lights were initially blinking at different locations through the city, but then the number of lights increased, and they started blinking in a synchronized manner. These are just a few of the thoughts and images we received as we set out to recruit adopters for Newark's streets.

Today it is clear that the Lord wants to replicate the street adoption model in cities around the world. He is no respecter of persons, and His compassion extends over the entire earth. Given these realities, we envision today that an increasing number of cities will begin adopting their streets for daily prayer, and that this same Adopt-Your-Street model will ultimately be applied to entire states and nations. When this happens, we will see a partial fulfillment of the prophecy in Habakkuk 2:14, which states that, *"the earth will be filled with the knowledge of the glory of the LORD, even as the waters cover the sea."*

Jesus promises to visit every "town and place" that is prepared for Him. With this kind of offer, wouldn't you want to have every street in your city adopted for daily prayer?

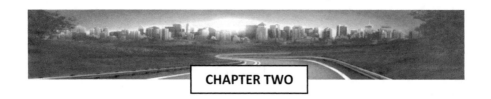

CHAPTER TWO

Prayer Evangelism, the Five Pivotal Paradigms and the Spirit of Adoption

Summary: If you have ever attended a Harvest Evangelism event with Ed Silvoso or Dave Thompson, you have heard a teaching on Luke Chapter 10. In this chapter we describe Prayer Evangelism and the Five Pivotal Paradigms, which together form two banks of a river. As Ed Silvoso teaches, the difference between a river and a swamp is the fact that a river has banks. We will see that the framework that has shaped the Adopt-Your-Street initiative includes these two banks and the spirit of adoption. This approach has become the trigger for detonation of the Adopt-Your-Street movement.

THE TWO BANKS OF THE RIVER

Ed Silvoso in his book, **Transformation: Change the Marketplace and You Change the World,** presents and discusses five pivotal paradigms for transformation. For years he has taught the principles of Prayer Evangelism from Luke Chapter 10. Dr. Silvoso frequently explains that the difference between a swamp and a river is that the banks of the river provide a framework for flow. In our prototype city of Newark, N.J., these two banks have implemented through two parallel movements. The first is *PrayForNewark*. The purpose of PrayForNewark is to mobilize as much prayer for the city as possible, and the ultimate goal, as stated in the PrayForNewark "Benchmarks and Vision" document, is that "every person who lives, works, or worships in Newark would be prayed for by name with positive blessing prayers in Jesus' name by an individual we can contact, and that person would know who is praying for him/her." The second movement is *Transformation Newark.* This side represents the paradigms for transformation and includes transformational churches and marketplace ministers.

PRAYER EVANGELISM

In Luke Chapter 10:1-9 Jesus gives his disciples four simple but powerful instructions about how to present the Gospel message. As Ed Silvoso states in his book **Prayer Evangelism**, we should "talk to God about our neighbors before we talk to our neighbors about God." Then we should share the Gospel using the following four steps:

1. **Speak peace to their household.**
2. **Fellowship with them.**
3. **Pray for their felt needs.**
4. **Proclaim that the kingdom of God is at hand.**

The PrayForNewark team has the custom of gathering on the third Saturday of the month to walk and pray in one of the 21 neighborhoods of the city. We begin with prayers of confession and for the filling and empowering of the Holy Spirit. We pray for protection for ourselves, for our families, and for preparation of all those that we will be visiting. Then we talk to God about our neighbors before we talk to our neighbors about God. Following a brief orientation to those who are new to our team, we review four questions that are useful in our meeting with neighbors:

1. *From your perspective in what direction do you see the city moving? How do you see the city's future?*
2. *What about your own life? What do you see ahead for yourself?*
3. *Is there anything that you need from God right now? Anything that we can pray about for you?*
4. *Would you like to have Jesus come into your heart and change your life today?*

It has been our experience that as we go out, the Holy Spirit precedes and accompanies us. Two quick stories: We were just crossing the street from the place where we started and came to a warehouse building that was being used as a church. We began to pray for blessing on the people who worshiped there and on the pastor. We prayed that their influence on the surrounding community would increase and that they would open their doors. Just as we prayed, the pastor opened the doors to the building and explained that that they were about to do a clothing give-away for the neighbors in need. Another time we were praying, and a team member sensed the word "foreclosure" in his spirit. They prayed generally about the neighborhood, and for the owners of the properties there. The next man that they engaged in conversation expressed his concerns and fears of foreclosure on his home. Because the Lord had gone before, the team had sufficient faith to pray for this man's situation and to believe Him for a breakthrough in his finances.

FIVE PIVOTAL PARADIGMS FOR TRANSFORMATION

The second bank of the river consists of five Pivotal Paradigms for transformation:

- **Paradigm 1: We are called to disciple nations, not just individuals. (Matthew 28:18-20)**
- **Paradigm 2: The Marketplace, which is the heart of the nation, has been redeemed and now needs to be reclaimed. (Luke 19:10)**
- **Paradigm 3: Every Christian is a minister, and labor is worship. (Colossians 3:23)**
- **Paradigm 4: We are called to take the kingdom of God to where the kingdom of darknesss is still entrenched, and Jesus will build His Church. (Matthew 16:18-19)**
- **Paradigm 5: Nation transformation must be tangible, and the premier social indicator is the elimination of *systemic poverty*. (1 John 3:8b, Luke 4:18)**

THE SPIRIT OF ADOPTION

As was mentioned in Chapter One, an early insight we received was the following: *"As you adopt the city and people adopt streets, businesses, schools and apartment buildings, the spirit of abandonment—the orphan spirit—will be replaced by the spirit of adoption, and the spirit of bondage/slavery will be replaced by the spirit of sonship."* This insight came as I (Joanne) was praying about the Adopt-a-Street project in preparation for one of the quarterly Street Adopters and Captains meetings.

It is the heart of the Father to love His children. God's father heart for His children is beautifully expressed in a compilation of scripture by Barry Adams that is available in the pamphlet called the "Father's Love Letter," which is available on our website (www.prayfornewark. org). Take the time to listen to or read this explanation of the heart of God. You will be blessed.

For more than twenty years we have lived in a small suburban community outside of Newark. In 2007, through a series of events, dreams and visions, my husband Lloyd and I were drawn by the Lord to join Him in a "New Work" of grace in the city of Newark. I am a registered nurse and I worked in Newark at the University Hospital from 1988-91. During those years, it was my custom to drive from my home to the Hospital's protected parking garage and back, hastening to leave the city as quickly as possible. As I drove by the boarded-up high rises and abandoned buildings on Irvine Turner Boulevard, I felt sorry for the city residents but was completely uninvolved with anyone who lived in the city. As a matter of fact, in 2007 when we sensed that God was inviting us to join in His work of grace in Newark, we knew just one couple and two of our church's mission partners (World Impact and Michael and Maria Westbrook from Greater Life). We contacted and met with each of them and were introduced to the Resident Ministers Association (ReMA) through Pastors Fran Huber and Frank Dupree, both of whom we had met through regional prayer ministry connections.

Although the themes of God as our Father and we as His children are found throughout scripture, there are two scriptures that relate specifically to this topic. Romans 8:15 states, *"For you have not received a spirit of bondage again to fear; but you have received the Spirit of adoption, whereby we cry, Abba, Father."* Then in Galatians 4:5-7, Paul states, *"To redeem those under law, that we might receive the full rights of sons. Because you are sons, God sent the Spirit of his Son into our hearts, the Spirit who calls out, "Abba, Father." So you are no longer a slave, but a son; and since you are a son, God has made you also an heir."* In both these letters, the Spirit of God seeks out His people and replaces bondage and slavery with sonship. It is the spirit of adoption that initiates this process.

After 1967—a sweltering summer that will be remembered for civil disturbances requiring the National Guard's intervention—there was a flight of all who could leave the city. Jews, whites and African Americans abandoned the city and moved into suburban communities. It was this abandonment that is now being reversed by the Lord.

As I began praying for the city and was received by the people that I met, I quickly developed a love for each of them, and more and more for the city. I realized that this was a two-way street: I couldn't adopt the city unless it adopted me. Maria Westbrook said it clearly, "You can't pray for us without us praying for you." The relational and spiritual riches in the city were exchanged for some of the material and motivational gifts that the Lord had given to us. Isaiah 62:12 states, *"You shall be called Sought After, the City No Longer Deserted."* As the spirit of adoption has been infused into the city by more than 1000 intercessors praying for streets—initially mostly from outside the city—the sense of abandonment has gone, and hope is being restored in God's Covenant City. This is God's strategy to rebuild our city: *"Not by might, not by power, but by my Spirit saith the Lord."*

STREET ADOPTION AND PRAYER WALKING

The term prayer walking, as popularized by Steve Hawthorne's book by the same title, is best described as "praying on site with insight". This is a powerful and useful strategy employed by many intercessors and marketplace Christians who have received a heart to pray in the power of the Holy Spirit. Many who use the term "prayer walking" have also embraced the land that they walk or drive through in a profound way. We like, however, to draw a distinction between street adoption and prayer walking by considering what is meant by the terms "adoption" and "marrying the land". In Isaiah 62, the prophet states that your land will no longer be *desolate* but will be called *married*. Ed Silvoso puts it like this: "Prayer walking is like taking an orphan out for a nice dinner and ice cream; street adoption is taking him home and raising him as your own."

For this reason we believe that street adoption initiatives grounded in Prayer Evangelism, the Five Pivotal Paradigms, and the spirit of adoption will have greater impacts on urban transformation than efforts that are not strategically aligned with these biblical principles.

CHAPTER THREE

Registering Your Initiative on TransformOurWorld

Summary: The TransformOurWorld website is set up to allow you to adopt any street in the world online using Google Maps software. In this chapter we show you how to get started by adopting a street, registering a prayer initiative, receiving training through multimedia Mentoring sessions, accessing existing content pages (through Blogs, Forums, and Groups), and collaborating with other users who are praying for streets in your community.

TRANFORM OUR WORLD ("TOW") Homepage

Go to <u>www.transformourworld.org</u> to bring up the TOW homepage.

Click on the feature video to see what's currently happening in the TOW network. You can download this video to your local computer if desired:

Adopting a Street

Click on Adopt your Street, then click on the video clip , "Why Adopt?" by Ed Silvoso. This clip reviews why street adoption is a powerful tool for implementing Prayer Evangelism.

WHY ADOPT?

You can get step-by-step information about adopting a street by clicking on the "Forms and Instructions" tab:

Q. How do you sign up to ADOPT YOUR STREET?
A. Follow these simple instructions:

To start, simply go to **TRANSFORM OUR WORLD.org** and click on the "Adopt Your Street" icon and follow the trail. You will be able to:

1. **Plot the street you wish to "adopt."** It could be yours, or one you choose to make "yours" – the one in your neighborhood, at your school, at your place of work - or all of them! Involve each member of the family in the process!

2. **See your "dot" on the map,** and see the "dots" of the others who are praying nearby you.
   Join a Prayer Initiative in your area. Use the drop-down menu to select the initiative that serves the street you have adopted.

3. **Start a Prayer Initiative.** If you do not find one that serves your "adoption," click on the "Request an Initiative" option in the drop-down menu and follow the instructions. We'll help you get started.

4. **Comment on your adopted street.** Who are you praying about? What are you asking God for? What changes are taking place?

5. **Communicate with each other.** "Follow" others' comments and let them "follow" yours.

6. **Expand your options.** Once you complete the Adopt Your Street registration process, you will have your own Transform Our World profile. From your Profile Page, you can expand your involvement and manage your preferences - anytime you want.

Let's see how to adopt a street—Springfield Avenue in Newark, NJ. Begin by typing in the name of the street and city you want to adopt. You can also type in the state, nation, or postal code. The map will display all the nearby streets that have been registered as adopted on TOW:

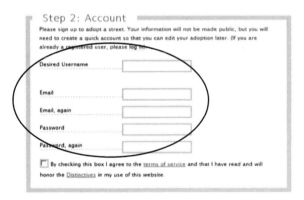

Next, you set up a user account by specifying a user name, email ID, and password:

Next, you are given the option to select an existing prayer initiative, register a new prayer initiative, or to save your street adoption request. In the example below, we have selected the Streetsville Transformation Network prayer initiative in Ontario, Canada.

Use the dropdown to select an existing Prayer Initiative:

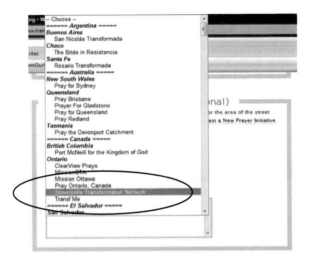

You can use the same menu to enter and save a new Prayer Initiative:

CHECKING OUT OTHER PRAYER INITIATIVES

Select any existing Prayer Initiative and see what streets are adopted by this team. The example below is for Transformation Maui (T-Maui) in Hawaii:

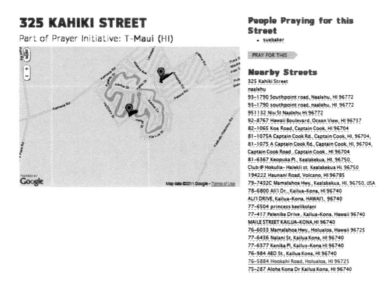

You can also go to the dropdown box for "Select Prayer Initative" and type in the Prayer Needs for your initiative. On the next page is a description of the Streetsville (Ontario) Transformation Network, including some of their major activities and prayer needs.

Streetsville Transformation Network

Currently showing 0 more recent adoptions out of 0.

ABOUT

Streetsville Transformation Network is a small group of believers with a vision to see our community transformed in all the spheres of life through the power of worship, prayer and holistic ministry in the community in line with the principles of God's Kingdom.

This is accomplished through:

Connecting Christ followers who live, work or worship in Streetsville and who share our desire to see it transformed.

Facilitating those who seek to serve Streetsville through community engagement in all the spheres of life.

Guarding Unity among those who love and serve Jesus Christ in our community by calling believers into biblical relationship with one another within their own local community.

Our activities include:

Regular meeting of pastors and other local spiritual leaders to build relationship and awareness of local ministries and local needs.

Monthly prayer gatherings of believers from several local churches to pray for the transformation of the community.

Encouraging believers to find a place of holistic service in the community where they can serve as salt and light by convening those who indicate an interest in launching new ministry endeavours.

Research into the history and present issues and spiritual dynamics of the Streetsville/Mississauga region to provide guidance to our prayer efforts.

FOLLOW THIS GROUP

ACCESSING MENTORING RESOURCES, BLOGS AND FORUMS

Mentoring: These are 30-minute video clips to teach you basic principles about Prayer Evangelism, the Five Pivotal Paradigms, The Spirit of Adoption, and so on. Each video is approximately 30 minutes in length and can be downloaded to your local computer.

Four options are available to you when you click on "CONNECT": Blogs, Groups, Forums, and Adopt a Street. Select the "Groups" or "Explore" option:

Under Groups, select "Prayer Initiatives" and then find an initiative on the map:

You can access all existing Prayer Initiatives (currently more than 300) from this webpage:

If you choose "Explore", you can get a listing of the registered Prayer Initiatives in the section of the world you've highlighted on the map.

Click on "Hopeful Signs of Transformation in Newark in 2011" to see what's happening in Newark, NJ. This BLOG section also includes a radio interview from WATV in Tampa, FL, which you can listen to in MP3 format on your computer, or download to your IPOD/MP3 player:

This will bring up a webpage that has links to recent events in Newark:

COLLABORATING WITH OTHER USERS USING FORUMS

You can read and comment on contributions by others in the FORUMS section:

Adding Your Own Resources

You can share your own story under the TOW Blogs section:

Uploading Data to TOW from Excel

Finally, you can enter names of several street adopters at a time directly from an Excel file. Enter the data in the columns listed below, then email the file to the staff at TOW. If you have questions at any time, just select the HELP tab on the right side of your screen for online assistance. TOW support staff can also help you with customized data downloads for your city or prayer initiative.

Last Name	First Name	Address	City	Region	Zip	Country	Email

CHAPTER FOUR

Developing a Personal Prayer Covering

Summary: *The Christian life is not intended to be a solo event! As you begin to adopt streets and pray for changes in the spiritual climate, recognize that we live in a world where good and evil are at war, and that your prayers are intended to push back darkness in your city. Begin by developing a prayer shield, and then proceed to expand your spheres of influence—at home, in your local congregation, at work, and on the streets of your city.*

START WITH A PRAYER SHIELD

The term "shield" is associated with a defensive posture. It implies protection from that which would otherwise cause harm, like a sunshield or a windshield. But this term is also used to describe a warrior in battle, on the offensive—for example with Roman or medieval soldiers moving with weapons in one arm and shield on the other. So there is an image of a conflict inherent in the term "shield". What, then, is a "prayer shield"?

Let me (Joanne) back up a bit and discuss why this military image is associated with prayer, which generally is considered a pious activity of talking with God. The apostle Paul in his second letter to the Corinthians Chapter 10:4-6 states, *"For though we walk in the flesh, we do not war according to the flesh. For the weapons of our warfare are not carnal but mighty in God for pulling down strongholds, casting down arguments and every high thing that exalts itself against the knowledge of God, bringing every thought into captivity to the obedience of Christ."* In Ephesians Chapter 6 Paul again uses military images when we are told to *"put on the full armor of God."* For present purposes let's focus on the prayer shield.

A "prayer shield" is a team of people who commit to pray for an individual who is called to work in pulpit or marketplace ministry. In 2007 when my husband, Lloyd and I sensed that God was planning to do a powerful work of grace in the city of Newark, NJ, and was inviting us to join Him, the first job that He gave me to do was to establish a team of people to pray for us as we embarked on this adventure. I asked and clearly remember writing down the names of 10 people as they came to my mind and then 10 more as I prayed for my husband. As I contacted those people individually, everyone agreed to pray for us in this specific way. These individuals are friends, members of a small group from our church, or others who know our family circumstances and have made this commitment to intercessory prayer for us personally and for the ministry work we are called to do.

As soon as we began to plan our first activities in Newark, we began to get calls from these people. As they were praying for us, they received a verse, vision, dream or impression from the Lord about Newark. These comments were used to confirm time and time again what we believed the Lord was impressing on us to do. We would not have been able to do the initial work that we began in Newark without this encouragement.

If you are involved with ministry in God's kingdom as a Street Adopter, a Captain or perhaps the leader of a ministry team, it's my strong encouragement to Get a Prayer Shield. Ask the Lord who you should invite, then be quiet, listen and write down the thoughts that come to mind. As you ask these people, depending on their experience in prayer, you may need to give some instruction on how to pray and how to hear from God.

Remember first of all that it is the Lord who keeps us safe. The Scripture says in Psalm 3 verse 3, *"But You O Lord are a Shield to me, my glory and the One who lifts up my head."* In addition to acknowledging the Lord, however, we are also called to pray for one another, and a prayer shield is a great place to start:

For You, O LORD, will bless the righteous; With favor You will surround him as with a shield.

EXPANDING YOUR SPHERES OF INFLUENCE: HOME/WORK/CHURCH

When we look at the people whose lives intersect ours, we can group them in several ways. We usually think of a *private* home as family and close friends and perhaps our neighbors; our *work life* is our office, our place of employment and the people that we are engaged with in that arena. This could extend to include what we call the "marketplace". The third arena is to borrow a phrase from Dietrich Bonhoeffer, our *"life together"*—the faith community where we are called to worship and to serve.

Of course we are called to worship and to serve in every arena. And our lives are also to be integrated. But there is a special way that this occurs in the life of a believer, one who is a subject of Jesus Christ, the King of Kings. *Two diagrams have been very helpful to me as I have processed these concepts. The first is just three intersecting circles with me in the middle. The names of the circles are home, work and church. The second diagram has a single circle in the middle, with ten or so circles radiating out from there. Right now, I just want to talk about that first diagram: three intersecting circles with me in the middle.*

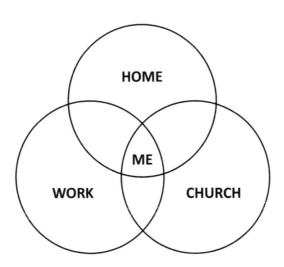

My *home* is located in the village of New Providence, NJ, which is about 12 miles from Newark. My immediate family consists of my two sons, my husband and pets. The extended family includes my parents, my sister and brother and their families. It could also include distant relatives, my husband's family and our neighbors.

The second circle is *work*, which includes a myriad of relationships in the marketplace. My office is at Morristown Memorial Hospital, but my professional nursing networks extend across the state and country. I work closely with another advanced practice nurse at the hospital and share responsibility for leadership in the unit with others. We interact with doctors, therapists, seventy nurses on staff as well as nursing assistants, secretaries, and housekeeping personnel—not to mention the 53 patients and their families that are on the unit on any day of the year.

This sphere expands when you consider the interaction throughout the hospital to include six hundred beds, more than a thousand nurses and five thousand plus employees. Inpatients, outpatients, outreach to the community, businesses, professional organizations, vendors, and committee work interact simultaneously across the organization. This includes our hospital's ethics committee, the training of resident physicians, and on and on.

The third area of influence is just as expansive. Our *church* is a place where we worship and serve. I have served as an elder, taught adult education classes, worked with a prayer ministry team, and participated in a small home-based group. The church has more than 800 families as members and many others associated through outreach ministries such as the nursery school, youth ministry, missions partners and adult ministry opportunities.

Another term that relates to sphere of influence in the word "realm". A *realm* is an area or domain: we have our home domain, our work domain and our church or faith domain. Now the word "realm" makes us think also of a kingdom. **What does it mean to be "as nearly as possible a kingdom of God on earth"? That was the prayer of Newark's Puritan founders. A kingdom requires a king, subjects and a realm. One aspect of that destiny ties into each subject, bringing** *all aspects of his or her spheres of authority—the home, work and church realms—under the lordship or kingdom of Christ, the King of Kings. We do that by praying as our Lord taught us to pray "Thy kingdom come, thy will be done, on earth as it is in heaven." We will consider the concept of the city's destiny in further detail in Chapter Ten.*

PART TWO

GETTING TO 100%

CHAPTER FIVE

Newark: North America's First '100% Adopted' City

Summary: In 2007 the Lord gave us a burden to begin adopting the streets of Newark, NJ, for prayer. Signs of divine favor began almost immediately. Two years later Newark became the first major U.S. city to have 100% of its streets adopted for daily prayer. Since then numerous "hopeful signs" of transformation have encouraged pastors and marketplace leaders to launch a wide variety of transformational initiatives in Newark and elsewhere. In cities around the world people are saying, "If God can change Newark, then He can surely transform our city!"

JESUS SENT OUT THE SEVENTY TWO

Let's begin our story by describing an event that happened in Resistencia, Argentina, in the fall of 2006. I (Lloyd) had just published my first book, **Highways of Holiness: Preparing the Way for the Lord,** and Pastor Alejandro Juszczuk from the church, Iglesia Rayos de Luz, asked me to lead a 2-day conference on this topic for his congregation. During that weekend we reviewed scriptures from Isaiah and other biblical texts that give instructions and describe the benefits to believers as they build up highways of holiness.

As I spoke, Pastor Juszczuk translated my message into Spanish. He explained to his congregation that the English word "highway" can refer to either a freeway or a street in Spanish, and so he invited his members to pray about adopting a highway or street in Resistencia. At the close of the conference, we invited members of the congregation to bring their signed declaration forms to the front and lay them on the altar. We prayed a blessing to them and then dismissed.

Afterwards we counted the declaration forms and discovered that seventy-two people had signed declarations to pray for a highway or street in Resistencia. There was a holy moment when we recalled the words of Luke 10:1: *"After this the Lord appointed seventy-two others and sent them two by two ahead of him to every town and place where he was about to go."* We realized then that the Lord's instructions applied not just to the ancient church in Jerusalem, but also to this church in Argentina. This was the beginning of our ministry to see streets adopted in cities around the world.

"TAKE THIS MESSAGE TO THE LEADERS OF NEWARK"

As God usually does, He began this prayer movement by transforming the minds and hearts of individuals He chooses to use. Romans 12:1-2 tells us to *"be transformed by the renewing of our minds."* My book, **Highways of Holiness,** was based on Isaiah 35:8, which declares, *"And a highway will be there; it will be called the Way of Holiness."* That book reviewed fourteen sites of past revivals in northern New Jersey and New York City.

In doing the research for **Highways of Holiness** I was struck by the fact that there have been four spiritual awakenings, or revivals, that have come to our nation, and that each one of these moves of God has had a major impact on the city of Newark. As I prayed about this, I began to see that God has a great redemptive purpose in Newark, which was dedicated by its Founders to be "As nearly as possible a kingdom of God on earth."

Then in 2007 I heard the still, small voice of God say, "Now take this message to the leaders of Newark." That summer my wife (Joanne) and I met with leaders from World Impact-Newark and told them that we believed God was getting ready to do a great work of grace in Newark. We shared with them scriptures from Isaiah 35:8 and Isaiah 62:10-12. Isaiah 62:10 instructs us to, *"Build up! Build up the highway! Remove the stones. Raise a banner for the nations."* And verse 12 gives the promise, *"You will be called Sought After, the City No Longer Deserted."* We sensed that this biblical promise for Jerusalem applies today for the city of Newark.

And so we worked with Pastor David Ingersoll from World Impact to set up a website for the "PrayForNewark Adopt-a-Street Initiative," and we committed to work together to get every Newark street adopted for daily prayer.

PUBLIC LAUNCH IN 2008

In January 2008 we partnered with Dr. Bernard Wilks from Dominion Fellowship Ministries, who worked with us to launch publicly the Adopt-a-Street initiative on Dr. Martin Luther King, Jr., Day in January 2008.

The Lord gave great favor to Newark in that season, during which the city experienced an unprecedented 43 days with no murders. On February 26, 2008, the Strategic Operations Council met for our monthly meeting and gave thanks to the Lord for those 43 murder-free days. We praised His holy name and thanked him for this early sign of favor following the public launch of the Adopt-a-Street initiative.

The next day the news media reported that there had been a murder in the South Ward the previous night, ending Newark's homicide-free period. A 20-year old man was killed in front of a bodega in the South Ward, just an hour after our team meeting had concluded. This news article went on to quote the Mayor and the Director of Police, who were disappointed that they were not able to claim February 2009 as a "murder-free month." We wondered why God had chosen to allow 43 consecutive days with no murders, then lifted His hand abruptly on February 26. As we subsequently learned, God did hear the prayers of the righteous for a murder-free month, but this additional sign of favor did not occur until 100% of Newark's streets were adopted for daily prayer.

FIRST YEAR RESULTS

By the end of 2008 the PrayForNewark team was disappointed that we had only found street adopters for 33% of Newark's streets. We believed that God wanted every street to be prayed for, and that some larger churches would catch the vision and quickly get us to the 100% goal. We asked the Lord whether we should take out newspaper and TV ads, but His clear instruction was, "Not until you reach 100%." So we were puzzled why only one third of the streets had been adopted after more than a year's labors. The answer came from a most unlikely source—Newark's **Star-Ledger** daily newspaper. On January 1, 2009, the lead article on the front page of the **Star-Ledger** was, "Newark Sees Sharp Decline in Murders." The article stated,

> *"The number of shootings, including drug-related attacks, dropped significantly last year, driving the murder rate further down. As of early yesterday, Newark had 67 murders in 2008, compared with 99 the year before, and 107 in 2006. Of this year's murders, 36 percent were drug-related, compared with nearly half of 2007's killings, police say. Newark's steep murder reduction led New Jersey cities, most of which either saw more modest drops or slight upticks."*

When the FBI's official **Uniform Crime Statistics for 2008** report was issued several months later, federal officials confirmed that Newark's 33% drop in homicides was the largest percentage drop in any major U.S. city. While Newark officials were quick to take credit for this unprecedented drop in murders, those of us who were involved with PrayForNewark saw this as another sign of favor and an indication that God had not forgotten that Newark is still His Covenant City.

A MACEDONIAN CALL FOR HELP

In Acts 16:9-10 Paul describes how he was led to travel to Macedonia to deliver the Gospel message. The scripture says, *"During the night Paul had a vision of a man of Macedonia standing and begging him, 'Come over to Macedonia and help us.' After Paul had seen the vision, we got ready at once to leave for Macedonia, concluding that God had called us to preach the gospel to them."* As our human efforts to get streets adopted started to run out of steam, we sensed that we needed to make a "Macedonian call" to respond to our prayer burden for Newark.

Encouraged by the favorable results and favor from the Lord in 2008, we pressed onward to get the remaining 600 Newark streets adopted for prayer. But by this time our core team had invited almost everyone we knew to become Street Adopters, and it was not obvious whether we would ever reach 100%. Members of our core team continued to meet with larger churches and other Christian groups, but we saw that most of the positive responses came from small, spirit-filled congregations. We cast the vision to as many groups as possible, but we rarely found that more than 10-20 people would sign up during a church meeting or public event. In addition, we noted that people were adopting the same, well-known streets that had been previously adopted. We seemed to hit a wall when 45% of the streets were adopted.

In April 2009 Ed Silvoso invited us to speak about PrayForNewark at the TransformOurWorld conference in Jacksonville, Florida. At this conference we shared the vision for getting all of Newark's streets adopted, and we issued a "Macedonian call" to the conference attendees to adopt one of our streets. The Holy Spirit spoke to many that weekend, and by the end of the 3-day conference we had reached 50%—a major "tipping point" on our journey to 100%. The 50 people who adopted a Newark street at that conference signed up to "see what they had never seen before"—a major U.S. city with 100% of its streets prayed for on a daily basis. They signed up for other reasons as well: Many were Harvest Evangelism attendees who responded to Ed Silvoso's invitation; several were African-Americans from Jacksonville, who knew and shared the same cultural background as Newarkers; and others were prayer leaders who had a burden for intercession.

All who adopted Newark streets during that season were blessed— first, by seeing Newark become 100% adopted and receiving great favor from the Lord in 2009 and beyond; second, by learning how street adoption can work in a major U.S. city; and third, by getting a burden to take the street adoption model to their own city. Since 2009 we have heard many amazing testimonies about how those who responded to our "Macedonian Call" for help have become catalysts for street adoption initiatives in their cities and nations around the world.

AMERICA'S FIRST '100% ADOPTED' CITY

In November 2009 PrayForNewark reached the goal of 100% street adoption. We had wanted to see this happen in October, so that we could go to the Harvest Evangelism International Institute on Nation Transformation and announce that our goal had been reached. Despite all our efforts, however, we again had to acknowledge that our own human efforts were insufficient, and so we boarded the plane for Honolulu knowing that we still lacked street adopters for 3% of Newark's 900 streets. Then, by the grace of God, the team at home received another surge of replies, and the last 30 streets were adopted during the opening day of the conference. In God's perfect timing, He provided favor to reach 100% in the middle of the international conference, so that we were able to glorify Him for His faithfulness before delegates from 29 nations. When the time came for our session on PrayForNewark on November 9, we announced to the world that Newark was now the first "100% Adopted" city in the U.S. There was much applause and thanksgiving to the Lord for what He had accomplished that day, and seeds were planted for these delegates to take the street adoption model back to their homes on six continents.

After Newark became the first major city in America to have all its streets adopted for daily prayer, other cities including Chicago, Cincinnati, Tampa Bay, San Antonio and Washington, DC, contacted us to find out how they could begin street adoption initiatives in their community. Other leaders from Bermuda, Thailand, South Africa, Argentina, and other nations also became "early adopters" of street adoption initiatives overseas.

HOPEFUL SIGNS OF TRANSFORMATION

During the Great Awakening in America (1730's-40's) revival leader Jonathan Edwards urged Christians to look for "hopeful signs" of the advancement of God's kingdom on earth. He avidly read newspapers, magazines, and personal correspondence to understand where God's hand was present in America and abroad. To Edwards these hopeful signs were visible evidence that God was at work, transforming individual hearts and nations.

Today we are flooded with a constant barrage of information from the news media, Facebook, printed publications, phone messages, and the like. Most of us receive far more information than we can ever process in a day, and so we never completely digest in-depth articles of significance. In addition, we know that the news media are biased toward "negative information"—wars, unemployment, personal tragedies, and the like—stories that professional journalists know sell their articles and products. *As a consequence of these factors, Christians may miss a lot of important information about where God is at work. For these reasons it is highly advantageous for us to keep written accounts not only of answers to our personal prayer requests, but also signs of favor that are happening in the political and economic arenas.*

Here is a listing of some of the "hopeful signs" that we have seen in Newark since 100% of the streets were adopted in 2009:

1. **Regional Planning Board proposes $15 billion expansion for Newark Liberty and New York City Airports (1/29/11)**—This proposal could save 130,000 jobs in the NY/NJ region.

2. **Federal Government announces the largest mob roundup in U.S. history (1/21/11)**—125 people are arrested in a multi-state sweep. Operations in Port Newark are included in these arrests.

3. **Bayonne Bridge Expansion to increase the capacity of the Port Authority of New York and New Jersey (4/2/10)**—Plan to raise the Bayonne Bridge may save 269,000 additional jobs in the region by 2025.

4. **Panasonic Confirms it will move its U.S. Headquarters to Newark (4/2/11)**—The Panasonic Corporation announces it will build its new U.S. headquarters in Newark. Local officials view this decision as "the transaction that redefines the city's trajectory" of economic growth.

5. **NCAA Eastern Regional Basketball Finals are held in Newark (3/27/11)**—These national men's basketball games held at the Prudential Center bring more than $6 million in tourist revenue and boosts Newark's reputation.

6. **Chicago appoints Newark's Garry McCarthy as new Superintendent of Police (5/2/11)**—Chicago officials and Newark Mayor Booker commends McCarthy for his role in reducing violent crime in Newark.

7. **Star-Ledger declares the Prudential Center to be one of America's top entertainment venues (3/22/11)**—In 2010 the Prudential Center was the 11th-busiest arena in the U.S. for non-sporting events.

8. **Time Magazine includes Booker and Christie in annual list of "The World's Most Influential People" (5/2/11)**—Newark Mayor Cory Booker and New Jersey Governor Chris Christie are listed among the 100 leaders who have had the greatest impact on the world in the past year.

9. **U.S. Secretary of Education says the eyes of America are on Newark's school reform effort (4/3/11)**–U.S. Education Secretary Arne Duncan states that Newark occupies center stage in the national education reform movement and can set a national standard for excellence.

10. **ABC News announced that Newark's "Turning Point" was the August 2007 schoolyard killings (4/8/10)**—ABC announces that the city's response to the murder of 3 promising teenagers helped galvanize community efforts to improve Newark.

11. **First murder-free month in 44 years (Interview with National Public Radio, 4/2/10)**—An interesting interview in which Mayor Cory Booker discusses the city's transformation initiatives in crime reduction and other policy areas.

12. **Alleged drug kingpin captured in Newark (4/20/10)**—One of the FBI's "Top 15" fugitives is captured in Newark after a year-long national manhunt.

13. **32-year old murder case allegedly solved (3/29/10)**—In 2008 after an Irvington man gave his life to Jesus Christ, he confesses his involvement in the death of 5 Newark teenagers in 1978. This case had baffled Newark detectives for 32 years. A PrayForNewark Street Adopter began to pray for the street where these murders happened in the fall of 2007.

14. **Marriott announces the opening of first new downtown hotel in Newark in 38 years (2/4/10)**—This is the first major downtown hotel to be built in Newark since the 1970's.

15. **New Children's Museum to be built in Newark (4/11/10)**—This is a most encouraging development which demonstrates that Newark is becoming a tourist attraction to families with young children.

16. **St. Michael's Medical Center receives a $250 million upgrade (4/20/10)**—St. Michael's, which was struggling to survive two years ago, announces that it will expand its facilities in downtown Newark.

17. **Facebook CEO announces $100 million matching grant to Newark School District on the Oprah Winfrey Show (9/24/2010)**. This is the largest private grant to a public school system in U.S. history. To date another $43 million in matching funds have been donated by private philanthropists.

18. **Foundations donate $3 Million to transform Newark's Military Park (11/2/10)**. Acclaimed developer Dan Biederman has been hired by 3 foundations to revive Military Park. He previously renovated Bryant Park in New York City, which contributed to an economic boom in that Manhattan neighborhood.

None of these events could have been anticipated in Newark even five years ago. In every part of the city, residents and visitors are noting that there has been a new spiritual climate since 2007—when Harvest Evangelism's team led by Chief Jay Swallow and Dave Thompson first came to Newark. We believe that God will continue to show us "greater things" as Newark's spiritual climate continues to brighten, one street at a time.

Through the videos, "Transformation in Newark, New Jersey," (Parts 1 and 2) as well as brochures and personal testimonies, people around the world are being encouraged by the work God is doing to transform Newark. Jack Serra, VP for Harvest Evangelism in the Eastern Region, was recently invited to visit a group of pastors in a small coal town in Eastern Pennsylvania. They had been praying faithfully for their city for years but were becoming discouraged by the lack of visible answers to their prayers. After listening to their stories and concerns, Jack asked them if they knew what was happening in Newark. Then he told them about the street adoption movement, the early signs of favor in terms of crime reduction, and the other tangible changes that had happened in Newark since his 2007 visit to the city. Their faces brightened up. "If God can bring transformation to Newark, then there's hope for our community!" Then these pastors pledged that they would stay in their community unless all agreed that God was calling one of them to move to another area.

Throughout the Bible God repeatedly takes the most hopeless, desperate situations and answers prayers in ways that demonstrate His power and love for His people. Recently a Christian from Egypt came up to me at a Harvest Evangelism conference and mentioned that he had heard the story about Newark's "murder-free month" in March 2010. He had read about it in the "Believe It or Not" column in the largest daily newspaper in Egypt. "The story of the transformation of Newark is impacting the nations!" he exclaimed. When he shares this story with friends in Cairo, he tells them the part that this newspaper didn't print—that this "believe it or not" event happened shortly after Newark became America's first "100% adopted" city. Transformation is happening today in Newark—and it is becoming a "detonator city" for street adoption initiatives around the world. God is taking America's former "murder capital" and turning it back into a "city on a hill"—a city that brings light to the nations—just as Newark's Puritan Founders envisioned it to be in 1666.

TO THE ENDS OF THE EARTH

In summary, as Harvest Evangelism has noted, no city has ever been reached without help from the outside—including Jerusalem, as recorded in the book of Acts. PrayForNewark brought in hope from the outside, which in turn released the grace that was already present in the city. Now, as individuals and churches in Newark are recruiting people to pray for every <u>individual</u> in the city, we are seeing the fulfillment of the promise in Isaiah 62:12: *"And you will be called Sought After, the City No Longer Deserted."*

Today, pastors and marketplace ministers are taking the street adoption model to cities and nations on every continent, and we are receiving encouraging testimonies about tangible results being achieved and plans to take street adoption to the state and national levels in more than 35 nations. ***As street adoption is being applied in the context of Prayer Evangelism and the Five Pivotal Paradigms, the Transformation Movement is taking the next step in fulfillment of the Great Commission—to go and make disciples of all nations (Matthew 28:19).***

CHAPTER SIX

Street Adoption Roles and Responsibilities

Summary: From our experience a citywide Adopt-Your-Street initiative will progress through four phases: (1) Measure, (2) Monitor, (3) Manage, and (4) Multiply. This chapter summarizes the various roles and responsibilities you may need for each of these four phases and provides an example of guiding principles to help launch and sustain your initiative.

SEVEN GUIDING PRINCIPLES

In 2008 the organizers of PrayForNewark defined seven core principles for our street adoption initiative. These principles provide a framework for our present and future operations, which helps current and prospective Street Adopters and Captains to understand their roles and responsibilities in relation to the goals of the initiative. These guiding principles are flexible and can be easily modified in response to changing needs in the community.

1. **Who can adopt a street:** Anyone who lives inside or outside of Newark can be a Street Adopter.
2. **Christian focus:** PrayForNewark is a Christian initiative, but a person does not need to be a Christian in order to adopt a street. The biblical foundations behind this initiative are Prayer Evangelism and the Five Pivotal Paradigms (as discussed in Chapter Two).
3. **Leadership team:** PrayForNewark is under the leadership of the Strategic Operations Council, which supports the Dr. Martin Luther King, Jr., Urban Convocation. Dr. Bernard Wilks is the head of this Council.
4. **Meetings:** PrayForNewark holds quarterly Street Adopters & Captain Meetings in order to encourage the participation and feedback of PrayForNewark members. We believe the City of Newark will be built up as prayer leaders support one another in citywide efforts.
5. **Goals:** The initial goal of PrayForNewark was to ensure that each street in the city is prayed for by at least one known individual. Goals will be updated on an annual basis.
6. **Commitment:** Street Adopters are asked to pray for their street(s) every day for one year. At the end of the year they are encouraged to re-adopt their street(s) for another year.
7. **Communications:** Street Adopters may be contacted to announce upcoming prayer meetings but not for political, commercial, or other secular purposes.

GETTING TO 100%

In setting up a street adoption initiative it is important to acknowledge that you are cooperating with the Holy Spirit to invite Jesus into your city. You get a prayer burden to pray for your city and begin going out with whatever resources the Lord has given you. From our experience your Adopt-Your-Street initiative will progress through a series of phases.

You start with a list of streets to be adopted and set up a process to measure your progress. This is the first of four phases of adopting the streets in your city. In phase two you monitor your progress and watch it expand until approximately half of the streets are adopted. In the third phase you set up Captains who are assigned to complete the adoption of every street in a designated neighborhood or district. The fourth phase involves multiplying the adoption process after you reach 100%. These phases are described below.

––––––––––––––––––

Phase 1: Measure

In this phase you get the first 10% of the streets adopted in your city. In this initial phase you establish your initiative with a small cohesive core group and a minimum of resources. You begin Prayer Evangelism on the streets that have been adopted and invite others from your sphere of influence to join the initiative. Initially there will be very little definition of roles and responsibilities, and consequently everyone will be wearing lots of hats! During phase 1 your cohesive core team members function as strategists, prayer evangelists, administrators, Captains, Street Adopters, Prayer Initiative Coordinators, and/or data managers. These roles are fluid and will change as new people join your prayer initiative. Remember to establish a *prayer shield* for everyone who joins your initiative, as we have emphasized in Chapter Four.

The key for this first phase is to define your initial target area—whether it is a few blocks in your neighborhood, a school district, a postal code, or your entire community. Once you have established your target area, you find a list of streets and begin getting *Street Adopters* to bathe them in daily prayer. In other words, **your initial focus should be on gaining momentum, not on organizing a movement.** This approach is exactly what Jesus instructed the seventy-two disciples to do in Luke 10:1-9.

Phase 2: Monitor

In the Monitor phase you will get 10% to 50% of the streets adopted. This phase begins as soon as you *expand your cohesive core group* to involve people from different geographic areas, ethnic groups, denominations, etc. In this phase you should begin having regular meetings (at least quarterly) and may have specific individuals handle data management, presentations to churches and community groups, printing of brochures and newsletters, etc. Your core group will likely develop more specific roles and responsibilities in this phase. In phase two you may also decide to set up a website to publicize your initiative and/or appoint someone to manage the financial aspects of your initiative.

Phase 3: Manage

In this third phase you go from 50% to 100% of the street adopted. In phase 2 you will probably find that most of the "highways" (major thoroughfares) and some of the "byways" (smaller streets) get adopted. But over time you find that people keep re-adopting the same streets, while others may never get adopted at all. To deal with this common problem, you can recruit a *Captain* for each neighborhood. Initially the Captain's major task is to get 100% of the streets adopted in his/her neighborhood. You may decide to offer incentives like T-shirts, bags embossed with your initiative's logo, gift certificates, etc. to Captains when they get 100% of the streets adopted in their neighborhood. You will probably see an increase in excitement when the first neighborhoods reach 100%! Over time the Captain's role becomes one of praying for Street Adopters and ensuring that all of the streets continue to be prayed for as the prayer initiative matures.

Phase 4: Multiply

The Multiply Phase occurs after you reach 100% street adoption. At this point you will need to identify and equip *Transformational Churches* to move from street adoption to praying for each person in your city by name. Additionally, however, you may decide to establish Transformational Churches in the Monitor or Manage phases, which can help to accelerate reaching the 100% street adoption objective.

Phase 4 is very important, since your prayer initiative may not survive unless you implement a strategy to sustain the effort you've invested to get it going. Because this topic is so important, the next chapter will discuss in detail what is required to sustain and expand your street adoption initiative. A summary of the four phases of street adoption is included in Table 1 on the next page. The roles and responsibilities listed in this table are defined in Table 2.

Table 1: Summary of Street Adoption Roles by Phase

Activity	Operations Council	Captains	Street Adopters	Prayer Initiative Coordinator	Database Manager	Overseer	Website Manager	Intercessors	Financial Secretary	Church Coordinators	Transformational Churches	Communications Director
Set Vision and Benchmarks												
Develop Signup Sheets and Fact Sheets												
Recruit Street Adopters												
Train Street Adopters												
Enter and Maintain Data												
Do Prayer Evengelism												
Set Up Meetings												
Run Tracking Reports												
Represent Initiative to Community												
Communications with TOW/AYS												
Receive Mentoring on TOW												
Website Content												
Financial Administration												
Recruit Transformational Churches												
Equip Transformational Churches												
Intercession												
Media Relations												
Churches												

Phase regions:

1-Measure (0-10% of steets adopted)

2-Monitor (10-50% of streets adopted)

3-Manage (50-100% of streets adopted)

4-Multiply (Everyone prayed or by name)

Table 2: Street Adoption Roles and Responsibilities

Role Definitions	
Operations Council	Defines Vision and Goals, establishes calendar of events, reviews all functions and activities, appoints leaders for key roles.
Captains	Recruit and train Street Adopters, ensure that all streets are adopted, and encourage and pray for Street Adopters.
Street Adopters	Pray for streets and those living on the streets. In Phase 4, work with Captains and Tranformational Churches to pray for everyone.
Prayer Initiative Coordinator	Works with TransformOurWorld and Database Manager to synchronize databases and mentors local team with TOW training resources.
Database Manager	Enters and maintains data on Street Adopters, Captains, and Tranformational Churches. Produces reports for Operations Council and Captains.
Overseer	Represents the AYS initiative to local churches, marketplace leaders, and news media. Member of Operations Council.
Website Manager	Develops and maintains website. Adds/removes content pages as directed by other team members.
Intercessors	Pray for Operations Council, Street Adopters, Captains, and Tranformational Churches as well as neighborhood/community needs.
Financial Secretary	Managers contributions and expenses. Prepares tax receipts for deductible donations as needed.
Church Coordinators	Represent the AYS initiative to a specific congregation. Inform Street Adopters from the congregation about events and resources.
Transformational Churches	Train and equip Prayer Evangelists to pray for every person in their district. Promote "righteousness, peace, and joy in the Holy Spirit."
Communications Manager	Keeps in contact with Street Adopters and Churches via email/phone/mailings. Develops/maintains presentations and meeting minutes.

GENERAL COMMENTS

Don't jump into an Adopt Your Street initiative without a thorough understanding of the principles of Prayer Evangelism, the Five Pivotal Paradigms, and the Spirit of Adoption (See Chapter Two). There are excellent resources on these topics in the 'Mentoring' section of the TOW website, www.transformourworld.org, as well as a wide variety of resources in the TransformOurWorld Bookstore. (See Appendix C for details.)

Let us conclude by making two general observations: First, you will probably not see significant changes in the spiritual climate in your city unless you follow Jesus' model for reaching the city, which is Prayer Evangelism (see Luke 10:1-9). Second, don't let yourself get discouraged by the size of the task at hand. Remember that Jesus loves your city and is waiting for you and others to prepare the way for Him to visit the people on your adopted streets. His abundant resources will more than make up for your limited time and talents.

The usual pattern is for the Holy Spirit to give you a God-sized vision for your city, and after that you will need to *"ask for workers for the harvest"* once you discover how large this vision is. If your initial goal is, say, to adopt 10 streets for daily prayer, be confident that Jesus will come to bless those streets. You will need to step out in faith, trusting that He will indeed come to visit your city. Once this occurs, you will find it increasingly easy to grow your cohesive core group and to expand the geographic boundaries of the target area for your prayer initiative.

CHAPTER SEVEN

Where Do We Go From Here?

Summary: Street adoption is a journey, not a destination. As a Street Adopter you are preparing the way for Jesus to visit your community. Whether you seek to adopt a neighborhood, a city, or an entire nation street by street, getting to 100% of your goal is only the beginning. After your have reached your initial goal, your Prayer Initiative is positioned to "see what you have never seen before." In this chapter we describe three stages of street adoption that will equip you to build and sustain your Prayer Initiative to support long-term transformation of your community.

AFTER YOU REACH 100%

Once you establish an Adopt Your Street initiative, you have taken the first step on a mission to bring transformation to your community. As the Lord provides prayer burdens and insights to your Core Team, He will reveal to you the felt needs of your community and what to pray for. In fact, it is likely that He will give you dreams that far exceed your imagination and resources. His ways are much higher than our ways, and the amazing dreams and insights He provides are evidence that these are from God rather than from man.

The ultimate goal in Prayer Evangelism is to pray positive, blessing prayers for every individual who lives, works, or worships in your community. Street adoption is model that provides an initial step toward that end. There may be thousands or even millions of people living in your city, but there are far fewer streets to be adopted. By starting with streets rather than individuals or households, you will quickly see progress in covering your community with prayer.

Your initial efforts in street adoption may be quite exciting, as you envision a community that is bathed in daily prayer and on its way to becoming a transformed community. You start by adopting the streets around your home, business, or church, and then expand to larger and larger areas as the Lord leads others to adopt adjoining streets.

As you work toward your goal of adopting the streets in your target area—be it a block, a neighborhood, or a city or region—you will need to move toward your goal in stages. Without well defined stages, you are likely to "lose steam" after the excitement of the initial launch is over, and you or others may even begin to question whether your investment of time and energy is worth the effort. For this reason let's consider the lessons we can learn about stages by reviewing man's long-standing quest to travel to the moon.

LESSONS FROM SATURN V

In 2006 we were debriefing at the end of a Harvest Evangelism conference in Argentina, and a friend of ours named Charlene started laughing as we talked with her about what we had learned at the conference and could apply when we returned home. "I have a word from the Lord for you," she stated. "I see the two of you on a rocket ship, which is going faster and faster. You are laughing and having the time of your lives." We thanked her for sharing her vision with us, but we didn't have a clue what it was all about. As we flew back home to the States, we prayed and asked the Lord what this vision meant. During our time of prayer, we got the sense that the Lord was going to use us to launch something that was different from anything we had ever seen before, and that he was going to do it in stages.

We reflected about the purpose of a rocket ship and how man's ability to travel to the moon did not start in the 1960's but instead unfolded over centuries through advancements in science and technology. As young children we remembered President John F. Kennedy's declaration that the U.S. would sent men to the moon by the end of the decade, and then we saw this goal achieved in a dramatic manner through the Saturn V program in July 1969. Let's consider, then, how man's ability to reach the moon progressed in stages.

In Greek mythology Icarus had a dream of flying to the sun. According to the ancient myth he built wings made of feathers and began to fly. As he flew higher and higher and approached the sun, the heat of the sun melted his wings, and he fell back to earth. Centuries later Chinese scientists developed the first recorded multi-stage rocket. During the Fourteenth Century the Huolongjing of Jiao Yu was built for the Chinese navy. It was a two-stage rocket that the propelled the rocket into the atmosphere and ignited smaller booster rockets before the initial stage of the rocket ran out of fuel.

In the 1940s and 1950s European physicists refined the concept of sequential stages and developed crude missiles that were used as offensive weapons during World War II. After the War the U.S. government recruited Werner van Braun and several of his colleagues from Germany to develop advanced rockets for the U.S. space program. Van Braun's team developed the Saturn missile program, which carrier the largest payload ever delivered into orbit. In 1969 the three-stage Saturn V missile launched the first successful Apollo spacecraft to the moon, and a total of 24 Americans traveled to the moon on subsequent Apollo space missions.

Stage 1: Launching Your Initiative

The Saturn V rocket used a three-stage design that was designed to get manned expeditions to the moon and back for the first time in human history. To achieve this feat, van Braun and his team needed to develop a stage one rocket that had more power (thrust) than earlier rockets used for military purposes. Five F-1 engines were synchronized to maximize the increase in velocity needed to get the rocket and its payload off the ground. As the liquid fuel was burned, the rocket overcame the earth's gravitational force and was propelled rapidly into space.

In street adoption Stage 1 activities include selecting a "target area" (e.g., a block, neighborhood, school district, or an entire city), developing a master list of streets to be adopted, and implementing a method of recording adopted streets (e.g., Google Maps on TransformOurWorld's website). In Stage 1 you may also develop a database strategy to produce desired reports for Captains and team leaders. Once these elements are in place, the Prayer Initiative team begins adopting streets and registering progress toward the goal of adopting all the streets in the target area. The detailed steps involved in launching and accelerating an Adopt Your Street initiative have already been defined in Chapters Three and Six.

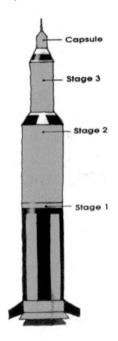

The Saturn V 3-Stage Rocket

Stage 2: Accelerating Momentum

When the first stage of the Saturn V rocket was running out of fuel, the second stage booster was ignited and separated from first stage, which was then jettisoned and fell back to earth. Having achieved its purpose, the first stage was released in order to permit maximum linear acceleration of the remaining stages and the Apollo spacecraft (the "payload"). The purpose of stage two, then, is to keep the payload on the same trajectory but with greater momentum. The stage two rocket was smaller than the one for stage one, and it was designed to increase the speed of the spacecraft to the point where it approached the "escape velocity" required to leave the earth's gravitational pull.

In relation to street adoption, Stage 2 begins when the Prayer Initiative team recruits and trains Captains for different sections of the target area. Once these Captains have been identified and trained, you can greatly increase the number of streets that are adopted per month. For example, consider a core Prayer Initiative team consisting of 5 individuals, who recruit 25 Captains to be responsible for different parts of your city. If each individual can recruit 5 street adopters per month, then the core team will be able to get a maximum of 25 new streets adopted for prayer every month. This number increases to 150 per month, however, once the 25 Captains add to the efforts of the core team members. Since the Stage 1 activities are already in place (listing streets, developing brochures and promotional materials, data management and reporting tools, etc.), Stage 2 efforts are concentrated on moving as rapidly as possible toward the goal of 100% street adoption.

Stage 3: Navigating Toward Your Destination

Werner van Braun and his team determined that a third and final stage was needed to reach the "escape velocity" required to leave the earth's gravitational pull. In addition, the third stage needed to be able to modify the rocket's trajectory to achieve a precise landing on the lunar target and to allow the spacecraft to return to earth at the end of the lunar exploration. The third stage, then, did not need to have the same thrust as Stages 1 and 2, but it required precise navigation to get the astronauts safely to a place they had never been before.

And so it is with city transformation. Transformational leaders need wisdom and flexibility to navigate to unchartered waters, just as the Apollo space team did. The best-designed space mission will fail if the crew lacks the ability to change trajectory as needed and maintain flexibility as circumstances change. Similarly, in city transformation the Lord must continue to guide the transformational team in a direction that will meet His objectives for the mission, whether it be prayer for individuals, creation of job opportunities, the elimination of systemic poverty, or other goals. Strategies that work well in Stage 1 or 2 may need to be modified in Stage 3.

In Stage 3 your Prayer Initiative core team will determine the gap between the master list of streets to be adopted and those already adopted. When one Captain achieves 100% adoption of his/her designed area, this provides encouragement to the remaining Captains. The excitement builds as one Captain after another attains the 100% objective, and these Captains are then able to redeploy their time and energy to help the remaining Captains reach 100%. The core team can also design incentives to encourage the Captains reach 100%—such as T-shirts, handbags with your team's logo on them, or gift certificates at a popular local restaurant. As long as these incentives are selected with regard to the team's mission, they serve as concrete rewards for achieving spiritual goals that provide lasting benefits to your team and community.

But Stage 3 isn't over when you hit 100%. Just as the Apollo team needed to conduct scientific explorations and bring lunar samples back to earth, your street adoption team must shift its focus to the specific mission that the Lord is calling you to perform—whether it be intercession, mentoring of spiritual orphans, job training, feeding of the poor, etc. When your team's transformational mission is achieved, you must also have energy and perseverance to do your "day job" in marketplace or pulpit ministry. For this reason it is desirable to designate term limits for your Captains (perhaps 1-3 years), so that the Captains maintain the energy and wisdom needed to nurture and direct the Street Adopters in their area.

SEEING WHAT YOU HAVE NEVER SEEN BEFORE

In summary, in Stages 1 and 2 the Prayer Initiative core team spends considerable energy building momentum for transformation. In Stage 3, however, the team seeks to reach the critical "escape velocity" required for urban transformation. In addition, Stage 3 requires continual assessment of the gap between the target (100% street adoption) and the streets currently adopted. To reach 100% efficiently, your team will need to develop data management and reporting tools to determine what percent of streets have been adopted at any point in time, how many streets are being adopted multiple times, and the like. Reliable indicators will help your Captains focus on how much your team has progressed toward the goal of 100% adoption, but you will probably need additional strategies and processes to train and encourage your Captains and Street Adopters. These may include:

- Using mentoring, discussions, blogs, and other collaboration tools on TransformOurWorld's website.

- Quarterly or monthly team meetings, featuring prayer, training, and team accomplishments to date.

- Special activities, such as supporting neighborhood events like ward rallies and block parties.

- Participating in citywide events such as the National Day of Prayer, the Global Day of Prayer, the National Night Out, and the like.

- Having Captains from one part of the city support other Captains when major incidents or needs arise (e.g., a fire or increase in violence in one neighborhood).

- Inviting guest speakers and leaders from other Adopt-Your-Street initiatives in your area or from another part of the world.

Stage 3 continues indefinitely—ideally until Jesus' return to earth! In PrayForNewark, for example, we spent 6 months developing the Core Team (2007), 2 years achieving the goal of 100% street adoption (2008-09), and 2 years maintaining momentum before launching Transformation Newark in 2011. The development of our current "Servant Leadership Team" is summarized in the following diagram.

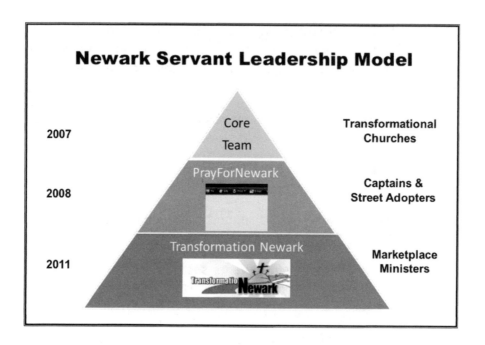

HOPEFUL SIGNS: CONNECTING THE TWO BANKS OF THE RIVER

The PrayForNewark Core Team consists of intercessors who have a burden to see transformation come to the City of Newark. These are transformational leaders who believe that Newark's destiny is to be "as nearly as possible a kingdom of God on earth." The Core team consists of mature Christians who provide leadership in different spheres of influence—e.g., pulpit ministry, marketplace ministry, data management, communications, and the like. This Core Team is not a fixed group, but one that expands as the Lord provides new "Transformational Churches" who offer leadership in wider areas of influence.

The Core Team, in turn, recruits Captains and Street Adopters to reach and maintain 100% street adoption throughout the city at all times. The Captains are mature Christians who provide leadership and pray for Street Adopters. The Street Adopters, in turn, are individuals the Lord calls to pray for one or more streets. Most of the Street Adopters are mature believers, but some are people that have not yet come to saving faith in Jesus Christ. The PrayForNewark Core Team believes that the Holy Spirit ministers to Street Adopters as they intercede for their street and the people who live, work, or worship on that street. In so doing, Street Adopters see daily examples of God's grace and deepen their own faith and walk with the Lord Jesus Christ. Numerous examples of God's answers to the prayers of the Street Adopters are being seen in cities around the world that are involved in Adopt-Your-Street initiatives. We will review several of these initiatives in Chapters Eight and Nine.

As the Lord answers the prayers of Prayer Initiative leaders, Captains, and Street Adopters, you are likely to see increasing numbers of "Hopeful Signs" of transformation in your community. As we discussed in Chapter Five, the term, "Hopeful Signs," comes from Rev. Jonathan Edwards' seminal writings on revival in the 18th Century. Edwards constantly sought to find personal testimonies, newspaper accounts pointing to God's hand at work in surprising local and national events, and stories about moves of God occurring in other parts of the world.

These "Hopeful Signs" are important for two reasons. First, they are answers to the prayers your team raises to the Lord during intercession for streets, individuals, and community organizations. These answers to prayers should be shared through one-on-one communications, email and Facebook messages, and quarterly/monthly team meetings.

But secondly, these Hopeful Signs are important in that they encourage other Christians to join your city transformation initiatives. As scripture tells us, there is a special blessing to those who walk by faith and not by sight (2 Corinthians 5:7). At the same time, however, there is a large proportion of the body of Christ—perhaps 90% in the U.S.—who are "pragmatists" rather than "intercessors". Pragmatists are those who, like the apostle Thomas, require concrete evidence before they believe something to be true and act on it. If the intercessor's calling is to walk by faith, the pragmatist's call to action is James 2:17—"Faith without works is dead."

As Harvest Evangelism as frequently noted, "it takes the whole body of Christ to reach the whole city." In short, "Hopeful Signs" form the critical connection between the intercessors and the pragmatists in your community. As the intercessors and pragmatists work together, these "Hopeful Signs" connect the two banks of the river—Prayer Evangelism and marketplace transformation based on the Five Pivotal Paradigms.

PART THREE

STREET ADOPTION AS A
GLOBAL MOVEMENT

CHAPTER EIGHT

U.S. Adopt-Your-Street Initiatives

Summary: Today there are more than 250 U.S. Adopt-Your-Street initiatives registered on the TransformOurWorld website. These initiatives are located in 30 states. In this chapter we review some of these current initiatives and summarize the plans and results that have been achieved to date.

Thirty U.S. states (including Washington, D.C.) currently have registered street adoption initiatives on TOW. California and Hawaii lead the nation with more than 50 initiatives registered in each state. Other states with 5 or more initiatives include Arizona, Florida, Kentucky, Michigan, Minnesota, New Jersey, North Carolina, Pennsylvania, and Texas.

Table 3: U.S. States Currently Registered for Adopt-Your-Street Initiatives

Alaska	Georgia	Kentucky	Nevada	Oklahoma
Arizona	Hawaii	Massachusetts	New Hampshire	Pennsylvania
California	Idaho	Michigan	New Jersey	Tennessee
Colorado	Illinois	Minnesota	New York	Texas
District of Columbia	Indiana	Missouri	North Carolina	Washington
Florida	Iowa	Nebraska	Ohio	Wisconsin

CALIFORNIA INITIATIVES

• **CALIFORNIA CANOPY OF PRAYER** — According to Ted Hahs, the California Canopy of Prayer is a coalition of grass roots prayer initiatives to mobilize Christians across every county, city and political precinct in order to change the spiritual climate in California, street by street. The objective is to see California become God's California. Above everything else the desire is to see as many people as possible come to the saving knowledge of Jesus Christ. The California Canopy of Prayer thrust calls on every Christian in California to "Adopt Your Street" at TransformOurWorld.org to become part of a groundbreaking strategic prayer thrust in our state.

California is in its most severe economic and social downturn with no human solution in sight; we are in a crisis on every front: material, motivational and moral. Without change, we are heading down a path of devastation.

Goals of the Canopy of Prayer

Change the spiritual climate over the state by:

- Ensuring that each one of the 58 counties in the state has a registered Prayer Initiative.

- Expanding it to the 430 incorporated cities.

- Making sure that each of the 25,000+ political precincts has at least 2 or 3 people praying and networking.

- Sustain the Canopy of Prayer until California has been transformed to be able to fulfill its divine destiny and the eyes of the unbelievers have been opened to the light of the gospel for many to come to salvation.

The California Canopy of Prayer has taken root and is growing. In the state there are currently 1473 streets adopted, 70+ local prayer initiatives with top notch local leadership, 5 cities that have committed to 100% adoption and are moving towards that goal, and at least 2 of those that are at or over 20% adoption.

• **EL CAJON** — One of these local prayer initiatives in the California Canopy of Prayer is *Canopy of Prayer East County, San Diego*. This prayer initiative is anchored in El Cajon by Foothills Christian Church, which is working with other pastors and marketplace leaders to cover their city and all of the east county.

"The Crystal Meth Medellín"

In 1987 when David and Mark Hoffman founded Foothills Christian Church, El Cajon was a troubled city. It was the world's number one producer of the illicit drug, crystal meth, and crime was at an all time high. Things were so bad that nationally syndicated columnist George Will dubbed El Cajon "The Crystal Meth Medellín" comparing it to the Colombian city, home of the infamous Medellín cocaine cartel. As usual, children were particularly victimized by the crime and drug culture. Many were in broken families and attending struggling schools. The city was not welcoming to churches. No church permit had been allowed for over a decade and in the El Cajon General Plan, the document used to determine proper usages for property in the city, there was not a single direct reference to churches. In other words, in the view of the city, churches were irrelevant to the future of the city and they had no plans for more. Now through the power of prayer things are changing.

Education Reform

Today more than 5,000 young people weekly are impacted through church youth meetings. Bible Clubs have been established on 24 public school campuses. After-school programs are providing one on one mentoring for hundreds of unchurched youth. The local High School Board is comprised of a majority of God-fearing Christians, and two Christian schools, a K-8 and a high school, are providing Christian education for hundreds of students at half the cost of other private schools.

Righteous Government

As Christians began to pray and get involved in the political process, things began to change. Christians were elected to City Council and began serving on the city planning commission. A God-fearing mayor was elected in an upset victory. A strip club and other so called "adult entertainment" businesses moved out, and churches moved in. There are now 60 churches that serve the city. Not only were they able to remove pornographic newspapers from being sold on El Cajon city sidewalks through coin-operated machines, but through their efforts led by city councilman Bob McClellan, statewide legislation was introduced to prohibit this throughout the entire state.

Decreased Crime

No longer the crystal meth capital of the world, crime has dropped dramatically. Property crime dropped 23%, domestic violence dropped 24%, violent crimes and homicides plunged 50% and are now the lowest in over 25 years!

700+ Streets Adopted to Date

There are currently more than 700 streets adopted in the San Diego region with about 200 of those in the city of El Cajon itself. This represents more than 40% of El Cajon's streets. Next objectives on their agenda: (1) Get each of the 764 streets of El Cajon adopted and (2) Reach out particularly to the businesses who have been hard hit by the economy and are struggling to survive. The businesses are very open to prayer, as is documented in this short piece from the local news:

http://www.10news.com/video/26178958/index.html

• **PRAY NOVATO** – Rabbi Miles Weiss and his wife Katherine, leaders in the Messianic Jewish movement, are instructing the Transform-OurWorld network in the foundations of the Jewish faith and the practical workings of that in a context of transformation. Today 20% of the streets in this Marin County community are adopted for prayer.

• **PRAY SALINAS** – After leaders in Salinas began praying together in 2005, the murder rate dropped to 20-year lows for two and a half years. They are now moving forward with an Adopt-Your-Street initiative and have 10% of the streets of Salinas adopted for daily prayer.

• **SAN FRANCISCO** – The spiritual climate is changing in this city that has long been known as a stronghold for anti-Christian values. Today 6.6% of the streets of San Francisco are being prayed for by initiatives in the TransformOurWorld network.

• **PRAY VALLEJO** — The faith community is partnering with a Christian mayor who has invited Jesus into the city. About 5% of the streets and 30% of the schools have been adopted for prayer.

FLORIDA INITIATIVES

• **PRAY FOR TAMPA BAY** – Tom Johnson writes, "Two years ago (2009) a small group of us began prayer-walking a 16 square block area adjacent to Bartlett Park in South St. Petersburg, Florida, a neighborhood known for its high crime rate. We blessed the land and prophetically proclaimed the gospel of Jesus to the neighborhood in the expectation that God's presence would increase over the area, the crime rate would go down, and that we would have a testimony we could take to the city's pastors and civic leaders—evidence that God will partner with us in blessing the city if its people will join together in prayer. We are pleased to say that God answered our prayers and gave us our testimony. During an 11 week period of Saturday prayer-walks, the average number of reported crime incidents in the neighborhood we covered dropped 46%!" Here is the rest of the story.

God's Promise to Us

"If my people who are called by my name will humble themselves, and pray and seek my face and turn from their wicked ways, then I will hear from heaven and will forgive their sin and heal their land." (2 Chronicles 7:14)

How it all Started

I believe God's promise. He WILL bless our land and cities if we pray. That is why, together with one or two others, I've been prayer-walking the streets of Tampa Bay's cities for nearly 10 years. *But never before had I asked God for proof that our prayers were making a difference. Two years ago we did...* But before that, I made two commitments which turned out to be preparation for what happened later.

First, we committed to discipling the city.

In Mathew 28:19 Jesus says, *"Go, therefore, and make disciples of all nations..."* Most people I've talked to about this passage focus on discipling individuals, one at a time. No doubt Jesus approves of the "each one teach one" approach to discipleship. But, thanks to Ed Silvoso of Harvest Evangelism (his book **Transformation** and others), we have recently dared to believe Jesus meant we are also to literally disciple nations! He wouldn't have told us to do it if it wasn't possible, right? Jesus told them to start with Jerusalem (a city), then go to Samaria (a region) and then to the outermost parts of the world (the nations). And that is exactly what they did!

What does it mean to disciple a city? For us it means to show the city (the civic and spiritual leaders of the city and its people) that the city can have a relationship with God just like a person can. God established cities for a purpose...so that His kingdom can be manifested there and the people can enjoy the blessings of His Kingdom.

Second, we committed to "marrying the land." Isaiah 62:4-5 says,

- No more will you be called Forsaken; nor will your land any more be called Desolate; but you will be called My Delight is in her, and your land, Married; for Jehovah delights in you, and your land is married. (Isa 62:4)

- For as a young man marries a virgin, so will your sons marry you; and as the bridegroom rejoices over the bride, so will your God rejoice over you. (Isa 62:5)

If we are committed to the peace and prosperity of the city in which we live, even as married couples are committed to the health and well being of each other, God will honor that commitment and bless our prayers on its behalf. For in Jeremiah 29:7 the Lord says, *"...seek the peace of the city...and pray to Jehovah for it, for in its peace you shall have peace."*

A retired policeman and pastor points the way

Something a pastor friend of mine said gave me the idea of demonstrating the truth of 2 Chronicles 7:14. Pastor Jay Brubaker is a retired policeman for the city of St. Petersburg, Florida, and as such, he knows all the city's "hot spots" for crime. One day we were talking about the city's crime problem when Jay mentioned how the local newspaper published the police crime statistics for every neighborhood in the city every Sunday. I began to wonder, "What if we identified the place with the highest crime rate in the city and prayer-walked it every week until we could show the crime rate was decreasing? If we could show that the crime rate goes down in an area after it is covered in prayer, we would have a testimony we could take to the city's leaders...proof that God will partner with us to bless the city. I asked Pastor Jay to show me on a map the places where most of the crime in the city was taking place. He showed me a half dozen places...all neighborhoods in South St Petersburg with names like Child's Park and Bartlett Park.

We decided to walk an old, historic neighborhood close to the heart of the city bordering Bartlett Park, an area known for drug deals, prostitution and gang activity. Our prayer-walks started on January 18, 2009, and continued every Saturday morning through April 11, 2009. During this time we were able to pray with a number of people, leading some of them to Christ.

Each week we tracked the crime statistics published in the St Petersburg Times. We are pleased to say that God answered our prayers and gave us our testimony. During 11 weeks of Saturday prayer-walks, the average number of reported crime incidents in the neighborhood we covered dropped 46%!

"...How long will you wait before you begin to take possession of the land that the LORD, God of your fathers, has given you?" (Joshua 18:3)

Let's do it! Let's reclaim our neighborhoods and our cities. We have the evidence. God WILL help us. Amen.

HAWAII INITIATIVES

• **E PULE KAKOU** — In October 2010 E Pule Kakou, a statewide prayer network, began a campaign to launch street adoption initiatives in every community in Hawaii. To date 50 communities have begun initiatives and are now registering street adoptions on www.transformourworld. org.

Here is a description of how they "hanai" (or adopt) a street in Hawaii:

CALLING THE CHURCH TO PRAY FOR ALL OF HAWAII

Encourage your people to "hanai" their streets.

1. This is not just "prayer walking" the streets, although that is a part of it.

2. To *Hanai* your street is to truly *hanai* the people of your neighborhood:

    i   Pray blessings and peace for them.

    ii.   Get to know them, fellowship with them, and find out their needs.

    iii. Minister to their needs through prayer and acts of kindness.

    iv. As God moves upon them, proclaim to them that the Kingdom of God has come. Invite them to your church. Share the Gospel with them.

3. Our goal is to "hanai" every street in Hawaii.

4. You can get ***"Hanai A Street"*** or ***"Hanai A School"*** brochures/ handouts by downloading the file at our website (www. epulekakou.com) or by calling (808) 839-4002.

MINNESOTA INITIATIVES

• **BLESS ST. CLOUD** — On Sunday, October 24, 2010, Pastor Mark Johnson (Jubilee Worship Center), Pastor Craig Moore (Life Assembly of God), and Pastor Bill Dornbush (Hope Covenant) brought their congregations together at The Kelly Inn in downtown St. Cloud, MN. After worship, Mayor Dave Kleis, who was out of the country at the time, addressed the audience via video tape. An offering was then taken which these pastors will give to the mayor, on behalf of the city, at an upcoming city council meeting. Pastor Greg Pagh, and his wife, Colleen (Pray Elk River) and Rick Heeren (Harvest Evangelism, Inc.) laid hands on the three pastors and their wives and prayed prayers of blessing and unity over them. Pastor Greg defined what is meant by a "transformational church". Rick Heeren spoke about being anointed for business and led the audience in prayer. Matt Pagh (Pastor Greg's son) told about the miracles that occurred when he invited the Lord Jesus into his insurance business. A video was shown of the positive change in the spiritual climate in Newark, NJ, when 100% of the streets were adopted. Rick Heeren showed the audience how to use the Adopt-Your-Street component of the Transformourworld.org Website.

• **BLESS MINNESOTA**—Pastor Greg Pagh and Rick Heeren have stated that leaders from Bless Minnesota are working with transformational leaders across the state to get every street in Minnesota adopted for daily prayer. Many transformation groups are already established and are listed on www.transformourworld.org.

MICHIGAN INITIATIVES

• **PRAY FOR FLINT**—Peter Schmidt writes, "We pray with the mayor of Flint every 1st Wednesday of the month, and today we shared with him the Harvest meeting in Elk River and the Newark Adopt-a-Street campaign. The Mayor was receptive to the prayer and to Adopt-a-Street and asked for a plan on street coverage as well as involvement of the church community to support the community efforts on the Cease Fire Initiative.

Let me give you our background on the transformation of Flint: For at least 13 years, the Lord has been strategically bringing to Flint or back to Flint, His people preparing the region for transformation. For me personally, I was called into the area in 1986. Last year when I was stirred once again by the Holy Spirit to deeper prayer and to Prayer Evangelism, I found out in August that there were groups of people praying for years for Christian Unity. We started praying each Tuesday with 1 pastor, 3 intercessors and myself back in September 2009. We now number about 12 pastors and ministers, 4 marketplace leaders and about a dozen market ministers as the group that prays once a week. Our prayer focus is to pray blessings on the city, repentance of self and church and leading us to transformation each day. New intercessors are joining us weekly, and our prayer intensity is growing.

I am now assembling the team of intercessors to stand in the gap as we prepare the material to present to the Mayor on how we will organize and who we will include. I have already informed the mayor that we will strategically map out the coverage of streets to match the efforts of the Cease Fire. I believe that our focus should be first on contacting the known intercessors. Most African American churches have intercessors and intercessory teams. These will be vital as we prepare to move on the streets. The Lord has led me to a man who prayer walks the prostitute- and drug-infested Dort Highway. Others are hearing God call them into rescue evangelism of people trafficing on Dort Highway.

As I put the plan together, I would like to share with you for your input and lessons learned. I need to know the mechanics on using street coverage electronically instead of by hard copy. Above all, pray for us as we proceed. I value the example the God has given to us in you, and I look forward to what God has in store for us in Flint."

NEW JERSEY INITIATIVES

• **PRAY FOR NEWARK**—This initiative began in November 2007 at a time when Newark was struggling with violent crime and fear in the streets. It was publicly launched at the Dr. Martin Luther King, Jr., Urban Convocation in January 2008. That month a 43-day homicide-free period began, and Newark led the nation with a 33% drop in homicides in 2008, when 33% of the streets were adopted for daily prayer. 100% of the streets were adopted by November 2009, and in March 2010 Newark had its first "murder free" calendar month in 44 years. In 2011 several new initiatives are occurring under the auspices of "Transformation Newark," which seeks to address systemic poverty, unemployment, and other major social issues in the city. Pastor Willie Moody's congregation has recently adopted the Georgia KIng Village

Housing Project and is holding weekly prayer and Bible study meetings in that complex. Pastor Juan de la Rosa's congregation has adopted all the streets in the Springfield/Belmont Neighborhood, and Pastor Gerald Whitaker's congregation has adopted 35 middle-school students in the Horton Elementary School. This fall Drs. Bernard Wilks and Lloyd Turner and others are piloting an innovative Youth Internship Program to provide hope and skills to teenagers who involved in the Essex County Juvenile Justice Commission youth internship program. See Chapter Five and www.prayfornewark.org for additional information.

• **PRAY FOR PLAINFIELD**—In June 2011 PrayForPlainfield became the 2nd major U.S. city to have 100% of its streets adopted for daily prayer. Under the leadership of Pastor Fran Huber, intercessors walk the streets of Plainfield at least once a month, speaking peace and blessings over the citizens of this community of 50,000. And their prayers are being heard and answered from on high. In May 2011 the leaders of 2 major youth gangs met at a local restaurant and worked out a truce to achieve peace in this community. You can read the details at:

http://videos.nj.com/star-ledger/2011/05/two_rival_plainfield_street_ga.html

PrayForPlainfield has prepared prayer guides for use on their monthly prayer walks. These guides are written in English and Spanish and are available upon request from them.

• **PRAY FOR ELIZABETH**—The Pray For Elizabeth Adopt-a-Street initiative was launched in the fall of 2010 through Liberty Center Bible Institute. More than 20% of Elizabeth's streets have been adopted for daily prayer. Their Adopt-a-Street brochure is available at:

http://www.elizabethsid.org/new/members/Liberty_Center_Bible_Institute/pdf/adoptastreetbrochurePDF.pdf

OHIO INITIATIVES

• **PRAY 4 CINCINNATI**—Greater Cincinnati and Northern Kentucky is a region ready to pray 24/7 for forgiveness, healing, reconciliation, and much more. So when Ed Silvoso introduced the Harvest Evangelism Adopt-A-Street model on February 26, 2011, to a capacity crowd of marketplace ministers assembled by Chuck Proudfit's *At Work On Purpose* conference, many hearts stood at attention, ready to hear the challenge to ignite our city in prayer.

In the 90 days that followed, the infrastructure was built following the models of Ed Silvoso's TransformOurWorld.com and PrayForNewark under the direction of Lloyd Turner. The Pray4Cincinnati Core Team has identified four strategies that will be pivotal in fanning the flames of prayerful revival:

1. ***Grow small to large.*** We know that since building this initiative, one community at a time, is critical to manage the rate of growth and for sustaining the prayer power, four neighborhoods are chosen to launch Pray 4 Cincinnati. Each of the four communities has a strong pillar of support: Colerain Township with multiple churches from several different denominations has formed a coalition with the Township government, area businesses, and non-profits that support individuals in need. Mason, Ohio has a thriving 'church without walls' that is eager to launch this initiative. Norwood, a 'city within a city' is an incorporated town completely surrounded by Cincinnati. Many strong Christian leaders call Norwood 'home' for the businesses they own. And Price Hill is blessed to have Cincinnati Christian University (CCU) within its boundaries. CCU is well networked in the immediate community and has a faculty and student body of spiritual entrepreneurs. These four neighborhoods will help our Core Team tighten the infrastructure and expand throughout the region.

2. ***Neighborhood Team Captains*** will be identified for each neighborhood. They will be able to leverage the relationships they have within their communities because they either live there, work there, or both. Also, Pray4Cincinnati has elected to try and secure multiple captains for each neighborhood. They will function on an equal basis and be able to assume responsibilities within their spiritual and natural gifts.

3. ***Video recruiting*** will be used widely to raise awareness and also to identify prayer warriors. A video is underway that will combine clips from PrayForNewark and scenes from Cincinnati. All footage will be against a musical backdrop of an original song by Dr. Ken Read from CCU. The song, 'Prayer For Our City' is both convicting and motivating as it sets the tone for Adopt-A-Street in prayer.

4. ***Building a resource library*** to simplify startup of the Adopt-A-Street initiative in other cities is high on our priority list. We are currently crafting logo designs, the video with the song that can be modified for other cities, a 'personalized' database system and more. And we want to give all that we are developing to other cities and towns who long to invite God's presence into their community.

If your city is interested in learning how to experience a rich, new experience with the living God and see how He is going to move in your area, feel free to contact us. Or perhaps you have found some tools or techniques that have proven helpful. We'd love to hear from you! For info on resources that could be modified for your city, email or call Paula Bussard. (Paula@JeremiahSummitGroup.com or 513.604.0075) For information on database management, contact John McCarthy (john@agimanagement.com or 513.379.8977).

PENNSYLVANIA INITIATIVES

• UPPER PERK PRAYER EVANGELISM NETWORK (UPPEN)

The Upper Perkiomen Prayer Evangelism Network, or UPPEN, is a coalition of 11 congregations in rural Montgomery County that are committed to adopting the 400 streets in their region for daily prayer. Headquartered in Red Hill, PA, UPPEN holds a monthly prayer meeting of all participating churches in Upper Perk and the greater Upper Montgomery County region. It is a time to humble ourselves, to pray to God, to seek God, to hear from God and a time to get new assignments from God for the region. Through the unity of many churches humbling themselves and coming together in prayer for revial, God is moving in powerful ways to bring transformation to Upper Perk and the greater region.

Churches in the nearby Lehigh Valley are beginning to note the impact that the UPPEN prayer evangelism effort is having on Southeastern Pennsylvania. In March 2011, 50 pastors and intercessors from the Lehigh Valley met and agreed to start street adoption initiatives in Allentown, Bethlehem, and Easton, which they hope will eventually grow to include all the communities in the Lehigh Valley. This is the third largest metropolitan area in Pennsylvania (after Philadelphia and Pittsburgh). See www.prayupperperk.org for more information.

TEXAS INITIATIVES

• TRANSFORMATION SAN ANTONIO

Nehemiah Initiative: Adopting the Streets of San Antonio

Inspired by the "Adopt a Street" initiative in Newark, NJ, we decided to launch our initiative in August, 2009, with 21 days of prayer and fasting in order to get more clear direction from the Lord for our city. We clearly heard Him direct us to take a "beach head" consisting of 162 streets in the neediest, most crime-ridden part of San Antonio, which is the West Side.

On September 1, 2009 a group of pastors, ministry leaders, a city councilwoman's assistant, and members of various church denominations gathered in the center of our "beach head" at West End Park. We worshipped and prayed and drove a stake in the ground, with scripture inscribed, as a prophetic act declaring that we were claiming the territory for the Kingdom of God. In the subsequent four days, the same group went and prayed and drove a stake at the four corners of the target area. In a matter of days the 162 streets were adopted and were being saturated with the prayers of the saints.

We were all in one accord concerning the essential strategy of prayer evangelism. We were focused on winning the war in the heavenlies in order to transform the spiritual atmosphere and prepare the way for the gospel. Another part of our strategy was to make contact with the pastors, since there were over 60 churches in our target area. We were welcomed by many pastors and launched a noon time prayer initiative Monday through Friday in a different church every week, praying for the particular church and for the neighborhood around it.

In August of 2010, we were ready to put feet to our prayers and were able to mobilize 400 volunteers from 40 churches in the city to participate in nine day (two week-ends and five weekdays) outreach to the community in our beach head. Most of the events took place at West End Park, which also had a community center and a large gazebo that we were able to use. Because we collaborated with the city councilwoman, permits were easily obtained. The events consisted of a health fair, job fair, a backpack give-away and free haircuts for back to school, and a talent show with participants from the community. We also had sports, and free hot dogs, drinks and clowns for the children. In addition, we had an outdoor stage where various Christian bands played and where testimonies and the gospel were shared.

However, three very important activities took place throughout the week outside of the park. These were Vacation Bible Schools at five different housing projects, door to door evangelism at the small businesses, and a house renovation for a poor family.

Marty Gaines of Ethnos Mission Center, who spearheaded the VBS, has continued his ministry to the children with a full-time staff of 10 persons, which is now funded by a large corporation. They have been provided with office space, which consists of two apartments at one of the housing projects and are literally present on site doing Bible clubs and other activities for the children and youth daily. They have been welcomed by the schools to have lunch with the children and provide tutoring for struggling students. They have assisted single mothers by attending parent teacher conferences and have blessed these mothers on Mothers Day with a banquet and gifts. They even organized an amazing Christmas celebration for the whole community last year.

Most recently Pastor Marty moved his church service from the north side to West End Park in the community center because he and his wife feel that these people are the ones they are committed to serving for the long haul. We have mobilized the prayer for the streets, and Pastor Marty as well as other ministries have gone in with the tangible love of God. This has dramatically transformed the spiritual atmosphere in our target area and beyond.

The Nehemiah Initiative continues to cast the "adopt a street" vision in the city in various ways. One local Christian radio station has provided us (free of charge) with a weekly half hour segment on Sunday afternoons where we can do interviews and testimonies to motivate and mobilize the people of God in the city. We also called a round table meeting with some of the more influential Christian leaders of denominational and non-denominational churches. Forty people attended. We were able to share the vision and give testimonies of the answers to prayer on the West Side. We have also been able to share at various local Christian events and have a sign-up table for adopting streets.

Answers to prayer for the West Side of San Antonio

Some of the answers to prayer have been:

- Gang injunction issued around the Lincoln Courts for 5 years.

- City demolishes an old foundation which was used to stage gang activity. Kaboom and Huggies donated $250,000 to the city to build a children's playground on the very spot where the gangs used to gather. The community was involved in the planning. Playground was dedicated in November 2009.

- Ethnos Ministries have begun Kids Clubs, engaging the children in the Lincoln Heights Courts. Recently, they have received funds to increase their staff and to extend their clubs to two more apartment projects, San Juan and Casiano Courts. The activities include Bible teachings, sports and games, movie nights (about 100 people showed up for the first one!) and evangelism. In one afternoon 33 children accepted Christ! Ethnos is now discipling them and teaching them about the nature and character of God.

- Churches are growing in their attendance. An outpouring of the Holy Spirit has taken place in several of the churches in our target area resulting in salvations, healings and deliverances.

- Numerous police patrols are rallied and walk the area from dusk until 2:00 AM.

- Large donations begin to come in to ministry efforts (over $275,000 to various ministries).

- 2 blocks from the prayer station, the city records one of the largest heroin busts ever.

- Land has been given to ministry by the Westside Development Corp.

- National Night Out event on the West Side (October 2009) put on as a united effort by various ministries in the target area won an award for the #1 National Night Out Event in San Antonio, the #2 event in the state, and the #3 event in the nation for a city the size of ours. Several people accepted the Lord, including two gang leaders. When asked if they were sure they wanted to give their hearts to the Lord, they said, "Yes. We're tired".

- Continued partnership with the City Council Officials in the area.

- A bakery in the target area, which was suspicious to the intercessors, was later raided and found to have animal sacrifices, drug sales and prostitution going on in the back room. The bakery was not only shut down but was actually demolished by the city with a television news report showing the bakery coming down.

- Hundreds first time decisions (many children and teenagers, four former gang leaders) for Capital Murder, Manslaughter, Arson, and Vehicle Theft decreased more than 20% in our target area.

- The San Antonio Police Department (SAPD) has instituted 2

new task forces, due partly to the prayer for the community! We quote from MySA.com: "Stemming from a rising number of prostitution and robbery-related cases, the SAPD recently instituted a pair of new task forces to bring those particular crime statistics down. The Calles Seguras (Safe Streets) project and the Robbery Apprehension Team (RAT) were both formulated by San Antonio Police Chief William McManus to target specific types of crimes while creating better communication between police substations throughout the city."

- Calles Seguras, a program being tested first on the West Side, aims to specifically reduce the number of individual robberies set up by prostitutes.

- Robbery Apprehension Team (RAT) was also formed. RAT is comprised of 40 officers that focus mainly on armed robbery cases, especially on the northwest and downtown sectors where the number of cases have risen. This collaborative effort has resulted in 51 arrests and 61 felony warrants cleared.

- More than half of 25 suspected gang members agreed not to publicly gather in a West Side neighborhood, making it a "safety zone" free of the drugs, violence and other troubles they were accused of causing.

- State District Judge Andy Mireles also ordered six others to abide by injunctions he signed, prohibiting them from associating with each other in the 1.5-square-mile safety zone, among a litany of other restrictions.

- Authorities seized a huge amount of uncut heroin and cocaine in a drug bust just outside of our target area. The really sad part of this story is that this is by a mother who considers this her "vocation".

Crime Decreases in San Antonio in 2009

Most categories of violent crime on the Westside decreased in 2009, and we believe it was due in great part to the united, focused prayers of believers! These are the stats:

- Aggravated Assault   down 5.3%
- Aggravated Sexual Assault   down 2.7%
- Assault   down 3%
- Capitol Murder   down 23.1%
- Manslaughter   down 28.6%
- Robbery of Businesses   down 9.3%

Some categories of property crimes were down also:

- Arson   down 20.3%
- Burglary Vehicle   down 8.7%
- Vehicle Theft   down 23.8%

In 2009 narcotics arrests were up 14.9%, which means that our police force were able to disrupt much of the illegal drug activity in our city. See www.ni-sa.org for additional information about the Nehemiah Initiative.

CHAPTER NINE

International Adopt-Your-Street Initiatives

Summary: More than 50 international Adopt-Your-Street Initiatives in 35+ nations have been registered on the TransformOurWorld website to date. In this chapter we review several current initiatives and early results from this growing global prayer movement.

STREET ADOPTION INITIATIVES ON EVERY CONTINENT

Street adoption initiatives are happening now on every continent. These initiatives have begun in large metropolitan areas such as Toronto, Ciudad Juarez, Cape Town, Johannesburg, and Brisbane, as well as smaller towns and villages in remote regions of the world. Some of the cities registered on TransformOurWorld are mature, cosmopolitan communities with major social and economic problems, whereas others are young cities like Redland City, Australia, where the population is wealthy and growing rapidly. In each city the common denominator is a desire to see a greater move of the Holy Spirit, a change in the spiritual climate, and tangible evidence of transformation occurring. Table 4, on the next page, lists the different nations where Adopt-Your-Street initiatives have been registered on TOW.

Table 4: Nations Currently Registered for Adopt-Your-Street Initiatives

Argentina	France	Italy	Portugal
Australia	Germany	Jamaica	Russian Federation
Brazil	Guatemala	Japan	Singapore
Canada	Haiti	Jordan	South Africa
Chile	Hong Kong	Malaysia	Spain
El Salvador	India	Mexico	Thailand
England	Indonesia	New Zealand	Uganda
Ethiopia	Israel	Nicaragua	United Arab Emirates
Finland	Ireland	Philippines	Zimbabwe

TransformOurWorld has a map that displays the last 500 adopted streets around the world, which looks like the graphic below:

STREET ADOPTIONS

Click one of the links on the right to start your search. Then click an adoption to see its details. Click and drag the map to explore, pray for adoptions, and adopt your own street!

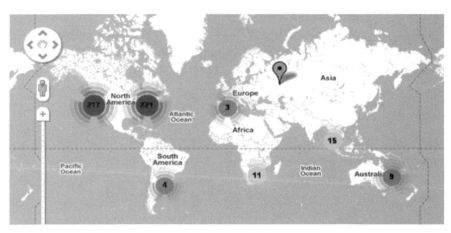

If you click on a particular country, however, you will see a display of *all* the streets that have been registered there. Here's a current display of streets adopted in the Asia-Pacific region:

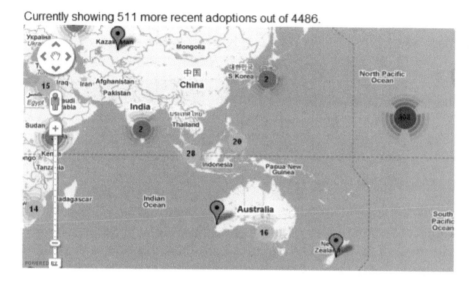

Currently showing 511 more recent adoptions out of 4486.

• BUSINESS BLESSINGS IN AUSTRALIA

In 2010 marketplace minister Wesley Leake launched street adoption programs in Brisbane, Redland City, and Sydney, Australia. These 3 cities comprise about 25% of the total population in Australia. He reports that Brisbane alone has 37,000 streets to adopt. He believes that 1 million Australians will come to Christ in the next great move of God in that nation.

• BERMUDA STREET ADOPTION PROGRAMME

Evangelist Joan Simmons writes in 2010, "We have already put all our streets, avenues, lanes and roads into a spreadsheet. It is a phenomenal job done by two wonderful women on the team. One is a lawyer and the other one is the owner of a trucking business. As we were praying, God showed to us that we need to do some Spiritual Mapping in all the Parishes before we endeavour to adopt all these streets. We are presently studying Arthur Burk's teaching on Redemptive Gifts of the

City. We need to identify what the root sin issue in each Parish is and also the Redemptive Gift so that we can uproot sin and then invite The King Of Glory to Come in. We are going for 'results' not just an Adopt a Street programme. Our Vision is to then call all the Pastors, intercessors, and politicians in each Parish and present this vision to them and have each Pastor identify a person in their congregation who will spearhead this programme. We will then train them, and in turn they will train the people in their congregation to prayer walk their area on a weekly basis. We foresee this being done by the end of 2010. I am tired of building the Kingdom of God on stony ground. We need to get those 'stones' out and build on fertile soil."

• TRANSFORMATION CANADA

In 2009 Derk Maat showed his pastor a copy of the video, "Transformation in Newark, NJ," and the pastor decided to share it with their congregation one Sunday morning. That day the text for his sermon was Jonah 4:11: *"But Nineveh has more than a hundred and twenty thousand people who cannot tell their right hand from their left, and many cattle as well. Should I not be concerned about that great city?"* After the sermon, the pastor showed them the Harvest Evangelism video about street adoption in Newark and then challenged the congregation, "And now what are you going to do?" During the next week this congregation adopted all the streets in their neighborhood. Two years later, this core team is part of Transformation Canada and dreams of getting every street in Canada adopted for prayer, starting with Toronto. They are seeing transformation come to their city—one street at a time.

• CIUDAD JUAREZ, MEXICO

Ted Hahs writes, "As you may know, Juarez is currently the most violent city in the world as rival cartels battle over control of the drug trafficking—it's estimated that 40% of the illegal drugs consumed in North America enter through Juarez. As this war has escalated, the violence has reached epidemic levels.

Adopt a hit-man

In response to the escalating violence, Poncho Murguia and his band of radical transformers have escalated blessing. They recently launched "Adopt a hit-man," to target the hit-men with blessing as an expression of prayer evangelism. Shortly after they launched this, God supernaturally intervened to save a notorious hit-man and bring him back to Christ. There have been various occasions where death squads have entered churches to execute hits; on one occasion during a wedding, the best man was the target and a stray bullet hit the groom, killing him on the steps of the church on his wedding day. Despite the risk the church unanimously welcomed this man into their fellowship anonymously. He is part of the church, but none of the other members know who he is. He is now discipling 8 other "ex-hit men".

Care for the orphans

They are also reaching out to the orphans. There are 15,000 orphans in the city, and each night 30 more orphans are added to that number. It was so moving to hear Poncho say, 'Can we care for all of them? I don't know, but we are going to try.'

Recently the church decided they would have no more parties for themselves--how could they party when the city is living in hell? Instead of a church Christmas party they went to the most abandoned school in the worst part of the city to give a party for around 400 kids. They are doing this despite the fact that the church is broke, because the violence is also destroying the city's economy. The kids in this neighborhood are so neglected that most have never stepped on grass or even seen a park, much less played in one. Many are orphans because of the drug war; this sector has born the brunt of the violence. This year there were two high-profile killings in which more than a dozen young people were killed on two separate occasions. One of these was a soccer team. The whole team was killed at a team party when a death squad targeted two of the team members. The rest of the team had no gang involvement or even knowledge of what was going on.

At the conference in Hawaii we challenged all the delegates to come alongside Poncho and his team, to adopt streets in Juarez, and pray with them for God to overflow His grace where sin is abounding. We specifically mobilized our intercessors to pray for this school leading up to the Christmas party they are planning.

Gang leader arrested and confesses

On November 30th, 2010, it was announced that police arrested the leader of a gang that has been contracted by one of the cartels. The police say he has been behind planning and ordering 80% of the murders over the last year. He has confessed to planning and ordering the two killings at the school mentioned above.

This is a small piece of good news in the midst of a horrific situation, so I don't want to be overly joyful, but if you need a sign that God answers prayers, I don't think it can get more obvious than this. We began praying for the orphans in Juarez and specifically those at the worst school in the worst neighborhood, and then within a week or two the man who in the natural is responsible for making them orphans is arrested and brought to justice.

To show the quality of Poncho's people: this man will very likely be sent to El Ceroso prison, the prison that has been transformed through the ministry of Poncho and his people. (It's actually the safest place in the city, but that's a different story.) In the event that that does happen, they are already making plans to visit him and lead him to the Lord."

• DRAKENSTEIN AND PAARL, SOUTH AFRICA

Gabriel and Paula Hugo have set up Transformation initiatives in Drakenstein and Paarl, South Africa, where Andrew Murray sowed seeds of revival in the 19th Century. In 2009 they wrote, "We are experiencing that the Holy Spirit is preparing our valley for Revival/ Transformation. Those of you who know the Late Dr. Andrew Murray will remember that a major Revival took place in our valley 148 years ago. We will commemorate this occasion in 2011. As we become more involved with the process of Transformation in our Valley, we are experiencing that we are reaping where we have not sown.

We have discovered that there are Christians who are already praying in the basement of our Local City Government Building on Wednesdays during lunch time. Our local Police have invited the Churches to support them in public solidarity, and they have permitted some of our prayer groups to do Spiritual Warfare inside the Police Stations. The Local Prison accepted us with open arms to minister inside the prison, and the Holy Spirit is moving in an amazing way with prisoners accepting the Lord Jesus as their Savior. We believe that *Government officials* are being influenced by the Holy Spirit. We are one of 650 cities and towns in South Africa, and we trust that God will help us to model Transformation to the rest of our Country. This process has just started.

As far as the *Schools* are concerned, we can testify that some of the mothers who attended the Argentina Conference last year (2008) are experiencing an astounding reaction from the school children. After presenting the Hawaii Transformation DVD in the first 6 of our 66 schools, 500 children started praying once a week for each child by name in one of the schools. We believe that the tip of the iceberg is showing. Obviously it will cost a lot of hard work to gain favour in all 66 schools.

In regard to the Business Community, we are amazed by the goodwill and the sincerity of many influential business people who are willing to contribute time and money for Revival/Transformation. As part of the process of Transformation the Pastors Fraternal of our City started hosting annual Revival Conferences. The Business community was challenged to support the Transformation action/process of the Ministers fraternal. The committee who took it upon themselves to manage the Revival Conferences consisted of fifteen people from the Business sector and eight Pastors. We think that this is an indication that the Business community is more eager to become involved in Transformation than many of our Church leaders. We have experienced that many Pastors are reluctant to relinquish their pastoral responsibilities for the Kingdom vision.

The good news, however, is that it was the *Pastors of the Fraternal* who embarked on the process for Transformation. Close to 40 Churches are involved, and although only one third of them are starting to see the light on Kingdom Principles, they have mandated the Fraternal to go ahead with the process of Transformation. Another positive for our City is that our local Pastors have shaken off a lot of the hindrances and burdens of our negative political history and race divisions and are keen to work towards Unity, although there are still fears that their personal identity will be lost. There is a very strong sense that interpersonal relationships are key to Unity and Transformation, and our local Pastors are making an effort to socialize together. We believe that the Malachi 4:5-6 and Luke 1:17 words about reunion of the fathers and the children are taking shape in these relationships.

Two main objectives which we need to focus on for 2009 were impressed on our hearts during the Argentina Conference. Both of these were supported by books which were handed to us by other persons who attended the conference and whom we met in Argentina during rotating between breakfast, lunch and supper tables. We were praying and asking the Lord for wisdom and insight for both these objectives. Without us asking for it, the books were given to us. The following aspects became clear to us: 1. Prayer for our City will be best mobilized by the "Adopt-A-Street" principles in the book *Highways of Holiness* (by Lloyd Turner) which we received from Lloyd and Joanne Turner. 2. Changing the Pastors' hearts to release and empower Marketplace Ministers in our City will be best served by the principles revealed in the book *Shepherding Horses* (written by Kent Humphreys) which was handed to us by Beth Steiner."

• ISLE OF SHEPPEY, UK

Esther Marsh from the Isle of Sheppey writes, "We will be raising a Canopy of Prayer over Sheppey on Monday 4th October. We would really appreciate your prayers not only for me in leading it but to encourage those taking part (very new for many people). We will be stationed at gates, the perimeter and the highest point of Sheppey. I am amazed at the positive response we are getting. One of our team had a picture of a giant bowling ball of prayer blasting through skittles (obstacles / strongholds), and it certainly seems to be the case that

God is removing opposition. We even have permission to prayer walk the perimeter of the prison on Friday 8th October."

(September 2010 email)

CHAPTER TEN

Reclaiming Your City's Spiritual Destiny

Summary: In the Bible we learn that individuals, cities and nations have a spiritual destiny. Your words and actions impact not only your personal destiny but also the destiny of your community. Tangible evidence of transformation will occur as you come into agreement with God's plans for your city and nation.

WHAT THE BIBLE SAYS ABOUT CITIES

For 1500 years Christians have had negative attitudes toward cities. Since the publication of St. Augustine's classic book, **The City of God**, Christians have believed that there are only two types of cities: The earthly city, represented by Babylon, Rome, Nineveh, etc, which is fundamentally bad; and the *heavenly city,* represented by the New Jerusalem, which is infinitely good. This paradigm allowed Augustine to explain how Christianity did not cause the decline of Rome, but to the contrary served to make it better than it would have been without Christian influences.

As we examine the Bible more carefully, however, we discover that Jesus did not share this negative attitude toward earthly cities. Throughout scripture, but particularly in the Letters to the Seven Churches in Revelation, we learn that earthly cities are in very different stages of spiritual growth and decline. In this chapter we focus on five types of cities, which represent five stages of urban transformation.

THE ROAD TO TRANSFORMATION

The Road to Transformation is a model that describes five stages of city transformation based on biblical examples. Each stage can be linked to demographic and economic indicators, which provide concrete evidence that a city is moving from one stage to another. A summary of these five stages, including biblical and contemporary examples, is included below in Table 5.

Table 5: A Biblical Model of Five Stages of City Transformation

Level	1	2	3	4	5
Stage of Urban Transfor-mation	Depressed	Distressed	Stable	Revitalized	Transformed
Spiritual Climate	Slavery, Abandon-ment	Broken	Hopeful	Proud	Joyful
Spritual Awareness	Widespread unawareness of city's history	Limited knowledge of city's history	Some knowledge of city's history	Significant awareness of city's history	Strong desier to fulfill city's history and spiritual destiny
Spiritual Reputation	Deserted, bad reputation	No longer deserted	Good reputation	Sought after	All tears are wiped away
Biblical Example	Nazareth (John 1:46)	Smyrna (Rev. 2:9)	Philadelphia (Rev. 3:7)	Laodicea (Rev. 3:17)	New Jerusalem (Rev.21)
Contemporary Example	Detroit, Ciudad Juarez	Newark	Philadelphia	Pittsburgh	Almolonga, GT; Adrogue, AR; Paranaque, PH

FIVE STAGES OF SPIRITUAL TRANSFORMATION

For several years I (Lloyd) was puzzled about how Newark had fallen so far from what it was originally intended to be – "As nearly as possible a Kingdom of God on earth." Then I reflected on a devotional by Oswald Chambers, who pointed out that God actually has two wills. One is His *perfect will*, or what He wants to happen. The other is his *permissive will*, or what He allows to happen. Chambers' key insight in this regard is that "the purpose of prayer is to know the difference between God's perfect will and His permissive will."

With that thought in mind I came to understand that the Puritan Founders of Newark had a brilliant glimpse into God's perfect will for that City, but over time the people of Newark took their eyes off God and lived according to His permissive will—what was right in their own eyes.

Then it occurred to me that there are five stages in the road to city transformation. These five stages are **Depressed, Distressed, Stable, Revitalized,** and **Transformed**. Here is a summary of each stage:

- **Stage 1 is a Depressed City.** *This type of city is "deserted" (or "desolate"—Isaiah 62:4) and has a spiritual climate characterized by slavery and/or abandonment.* The city has a negative reputation and may be the butt of jokes inside and outside the nation. The major indicator of a depressed city is that most people living in the city would leave if they had the opportunity. In addition, the city has "no boundaries" in terms of crime, corruption, finances, honoring of contracts, and/or human rights. Accordingly, there may be high levels of violent and nonviolent crime, a culture of poverty, and great social injustices. A biblical example of this type of city is **Nazareth**, and current examples include Detroit and Ciudad Juarez in North America.

- **Stage 2 is a Distressed City.** A Distressed City is "broken" but "no longer deserted" (Isaiah 62:4,12). It has defined boundaries, but they may be compromised in several ways. The major indicator is that a distressed city continues to lose its middle class population, so that there is an unstable demographic base. This in turn may cause the city's economic base to decline, resulting in chronic budgetary problems. People move into the area, work hard to improve their financial status, and then move to other areas when they have enough resources to do so. Those who remain in poverty stay there and may have friction with racial or ethnic groups that they believe are "taking the good jobs away from them." The middle class may be leaving for a variety of reasons: limited job opportunities, social unrest, crime, poor schools, etc. Widespread political corruption may exacerbate the plight of residents in a distressed city. There is a distinct negative spiritual climate in this type of city, but community leaders may be resigned to maintaining the status quo, which provides material benefits for the political and economic elite in this type of city. The rationale for maintaining the status quo is that "things have always been this way in our community." A biblical example is **Smyrna** (Revelation 2:9), and a contemporary example is Newark.

- **Stage 3 is a Stable City.** A Stable City is "hopeful" for the future. It has a stable middle class, a good reputation, a strong economic base and municipal finances, and good law enforcement. In addition, it may have several community leaders who are actively working to eliminate poverty, corruption, and social injustice. Still, there may be "bad areas" of the city which remain distressed for years or even decades. People move into the city for job opportunities, but approximately the same number leave each year. As a result, the stable city grows at about the same rate as other cities in its region. A biblical example is the ancient city of **Philadelphia** (Revelation 1:7), and a current example might be Philadelphia, Pennsylvania.

- **Stage 4 is a Revitalized City.** A Revitalized City is "proud"—proud of its economic achievements, its reputation, its innovation, and perhaps its cultural and educational advantages. The Bible describes this type of city as "sought after" (Isaiah 62:12). It is a city that is attractive to young professionals and others who have many choices of places to live. It will likely have an expanding economic base due to new industries or strong growth in existing industries, and it may also be a leader in business innovation. In addition, there may be many influential leaders who are working in the city to eliminate poverty, corruption, and social injustices. But its pride is both a strength and a weakness. Community pride is certainly a positive attribute, but pride may also blind the city to its spiritual destiny and resources. As people rise in economic and social status, they may become self-sufficient and fail to acknowledge that they are recipients of God's grace and favor. A biblical example of this type of city is **Laodicea**, which Revelation 3:17 describes as "neither hot nor cold" in regard to spiritual matters. A contemporary example might be Pittsburgh, which was recently selected as the site for the G20 economic meetings for its progress in economic revitalization. The revitalized city may continue to have long-standing corruption, poverty, and social injustices but may deny that these are major social issues. Tragically, the Bible says that God will spit this city out of His mouth if it continues to be lukewarm in regard to spiritual matters (Revelation 3:16).

- **Stage 5 is a Transformed City.** A Transformed City is "joyful"— thankful to God for His love and grace to His people. It is keenly aware of its history and spiritual destiny and is attractive to people in all economic groups. In this city systemic poverty, corruption, and social injustices have been (or are being) removed for all groups. The biblical model is the New Jerusalem (Revelation 21), where the presence of God is manifest continually. According to the Bible, in this city all tears are wiped away (Isaiah 25:8), and there are *"no needy persons"* (Acts 2:45). Residents in this city have a strong work ethic, and there is little need for law enforcement, because the city is free from crime and corruption (Habakkuk 2:9-14). A biblical example was the early church in **Jerusalem**, where everyone was *"praising God and enjoying the favor of all the people".* (Acts 2:47). Although there is no perfect example of the New Jerusalem on earth at present, there have been several approximations to the Transformed City in history. Contemporary examples include Almolonga, Guatemala; Adrogue, Argentina; and Parañaque, Philippines. Other examples in history included Newark (late 1600's), Herrnhut, Germany (1700's), Glasgow, Scotland (1820's), New York City (1857-58), the Hawaiian Islands (late 19th Century). Geneva, Switzerland, also exhibited many of the characteristics of a Transformed City during the Protestant Reformation (1560's).

These five stages of transformation are illustrated for Newark in the Table below:

Newark has been through all 5 stages of transformation—in reverse order!

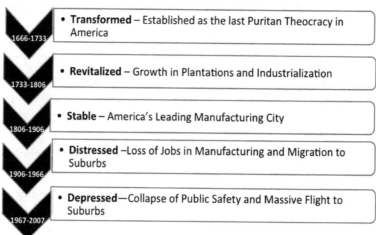

- **Transformed** – Established as the last Puritan Theocracy in America *(1666-1733)*
- **Revitalized** – Growth in Plantations and Industrialization *(1733-1806)*
- **Stable** – America's Leading Manufacturing City *(1806-1906)*
- **Distressed** – Loss of Jobs in Manufacturing and Migration to Suburbs *(1906-1966)*
- **Depressed** – Collapse of Public Safety and Massive Flight to Suburbs *(1967-2007)*

NEWARK REDISCOVERS ITS SPIRITUAL DESTINY

Like the Israelites during the time described in the Book of Judges, the leaders of Newark *"did what was right in their own eyes"* (Judges 21:25) for most of the 20th Century. The results were disastrous. During the past century Newark was labeled as "the bootlegging capital of the United States", "the worst city in America," and "America's Most Dangerous City". For years, skeptical outsiders asked the question, "Can anything good come out of Newark?" The news stories about Newark were almost always bad news—corruption, crime, poverty, and misery in a city that was once declared to be "as nearly as possible a kingdom of God on earth" by its Puritan founders.

But now a new wind of the Holy Spirit is blowing through Newark, as the leaders and people rediscover that their city is still a "city on a hill", and that Newark is beginning to manifest the hallmarks of the Kingdom of God—"righteousness, peace, and joy in the Holy Spirit" (Romans 14:17).

Violent crime in Newark is down 80% since its peak in 1995, and in 2009 Newark dropped off the list of "America's Most Dangerous Cities" for the first time in two decades. Today even the national news media are taking note that Newark is undergoing a transformation of historic proportions.

In 2010 the CEO of Facebook, Mark Zuckerberg, announced on the Oprah Winfrey show that he is committed to making a matching grant of $100,000,000 to bring transformation to Newark's school system. His offer was quickly supplemented by donations from Microsoft Founder Bill Gates and several other major philanthropists, and more than $43,000,000 of matching donations have already been pledged by others who want to "see what they have never seen before" in public education.

Like Zaccheus in Jesus' day, Zuckerberg is releasing his wealth to achieve Kingdom purposes. By stating that Newark Mayor Cory Booker and New Jersey Governor Chris Christie are the best qualified people in America to lead the reform of our urban schools, he is offering favor to Newark and to New Jersey's two most prominent Christian politicians. Oprah Winfrey responded to Zuckerberg's offer by providing free television air time to tell the nation that yes, something good can indeed come out of Newark.

Booker and Christie are counting on Newark's citizens to support this unprecedented effort to create a model of urban school transformation that can be adopted by other U.S. cities. Prior to becoming Governor of New Jersey in January 2010, Chris Christie developed his reputation as the Federal Prosecutor who won 137 consecutive cases against crime and corruption in the Garden State. Cory Booker, on the other hand, has become nationally known for his successful efforts to reduce homicides and shootings in Newark during the past three years. These Christian leaders have developed reputations for bringing righteousness and peace to the Garden State.

Thousands of intercessors for Newark are adding the third ingredient— joy in the Holy Spirit. More than 1000 people are signed up to pray for Newark's streets daily through PrayForNewark, and 21 Trans-formational Churches are being engaged to take the prayer movement to every person who lives, works, and worships in Newark. Christian organizations in Newark provide food, shelter, job training, family counseling, and other valuable services as they seek to infuse hope by addressing felt needs. These three key attributes—righteousness, peace, and joy—are the practical manifestations of the Kingdom of God, which we will not see in full until Jesus' return.

Like the ancient Greeks, Newark was adrift at sea as long as its leaders chose to navigate by their own celestial objects. Like the Greeks, however, Newark is learning to focus on the true North Star—and this refocusing on Jesus Christ and the Kingdom of God is making all the difference.

Facebook CEO Mark Zuckerberg and Oprah Winfrey meeting with New Jersey Governor Chris Christie and Newark Mayor Cory Booker to announce a $100 Million matching grant to transform Newark's schools (9/24/10)

Appendix A:

Transformation Principles in
The 1857-1858 PRAYER REVIVAL

In 1856-57 two thousand unnamed individuals began a program of 'systematic visitation of the poor' in New York City. These intercessors ministered on every block on Manhattan Island, beginning with the poorest sections of the city and eventually reaching even the wealthy class on Fifth Avenue. One of these two thousand intercessors was a marketplace minister named Jeremiah Lanphier, who is widely recognized as the man God used to ignite the New York Prayer Revival on September 21, 1857.

Transformation Principles in the 1857-58 Prayer Revival

It has been said that every great move of God builds upon past spiritual awakenings. For this reason it is not surprising to find that the Transformation Movement of the 21st Century owes much to the Great Awakenings that have brought spiritual refreshment to the United States and other nations in previous centuries. In this appendix we examine the role of transformation principles in the New York Prayer Revival of 1857-58, which some historians consider to have been the most significant revival period in American history. *In particular, we will show how the application of Prayer Evangelism principles prepared New York and Brooklyn for the mighty move of God that began with the Fulton Street Noon Prayer Meetings in the fall of 1857.*

THOMAS CHALMERS' ST. JOHNS EXPERIMENT

Thomas Chalmers was a gifted child who entered St. Andrew's University in Scotland at age 11. After a short time at the University he became one of the greatest mathematicians of his day, and he went on to become the most popular Christian speaker and writer in the English-speaking world.

In 1819, at the age of 39, he became the pastor of the St. John's parish in Glasgow, Scotland, which contained 21,000 people in one of the roughest and poorest sections of the city. At St. John's he implemented a model of parish ministry that was based on the conviction that the Gospel message is intended to produce social transformation. His Nineteenth-Century model "war on poverty" was predicated on the belief that the solution to poverty was not found in the liberality of the rich, but rather in the hearts and habits of the poor.

Chalmers started a wide range of social programs that included wash houses, cleaning of streets, helping the poor, removal of rubbish, sewage management, and other essential public services. *After three years government social services spending on these programs dropped 80%—from 1400 pounds per annum to 280 pounds per annum for the St. Johns parish. At this beginning of his experiment only wealthy families could send their children to expensive private families, but eight years later virtually all children could attend a parish school in St. Johns.*

He also began a series of "businessman's lunch" meetings that drew more than 2000 participants—a precursor to the Noon Prayer Meetings in Boston and New York in the 1850's. In addition he started several evening Sabbath Schools (which served as a prototype for today's "Sunday schools") and a system called 'systematic visitation' which was designed to bring biblical teaching to every house in the St. John's parish. Through this visitation program Chalmers and his 'visitors' taught principles of financial planning and household management, family worship guidelines, care for orphans, and wash houses where the poor could clean themselves and their clothes.

Chalmers' experiment in 'systematic visitation' became known throughout the English-speaking world as a practical way to supplement the Poor Laws that were being passed by Parliament at that time. In time the fruit of the St. Johns experiment became known across the Atlantic and came to the attention of the Superintendent of the New York Sunday School Union.

SYSTEMATIC VISITATION IN NEW YORK AND BROOKLYN

In 1855 Superintendent Robert G. Pardee met with leaders from the New York and Brooklyn Sunday School Unions and proposed a plan of 'systematic visitation' in those two cities (which did not merge to become boroughs of New York City until 1898). The plan included the following major components:

1. *Divide the entire city, county, or town into distinct districts, each comprising a definite territory, having reference to the number and size of Evangelical Christian churches in the vicinity.*

2. *Request that each church take a district and become responsible for permanent visitation of the residents of that district.*

3. *Send the visitors out two by two to the district for the purpose of visiting each household. If possible, bring each child and youth into a Sabbath school and encourage each family to attend some place of worship.*

4. *Each visitor will become personally responsible for visiting every family in his or her district at least once a month.*

5. *Each church should set aside one of the weekly prayer meetings for the sharing of reports and prayers for the church's visitation program*

In the fall of 1856 several churches in these cities agreed to participate in these initiatives, and within two years more than 4000 'visitors' were commissioned to do house-to-house systematic visitation of the areas assigned to them by the New York and Brooklyn Sunday School Unions.

JEREMIAH LANPHIER AS A PRAYER EVANGELIST

In July of 1857 a businessman named Jeremiah Lanphier accepted a position to lead the systematic visitation effort for the Fulton Street Dutch Reformed Church in New York. His specific assignment was to do house-to-house visitation, to distribute tracts, and to pray for businessmen as they went about their activities on lower Wall Street. He was one of 2000 'visitors' that were recruited to cover New York City with prayer under the auspices of the New York Sabbath School Union and the Dutch Reformed Church.

In September of that year the Holy Spirit prevailed upon Lanphier to start what many other Christian leaders had unsuccessfully tried to do in New York—to organize a sustainable Noon-Prayer meeting for businessmen. Dozens of noon prayer meetings had been set up in previously, but these efforts typically started in the fall and disbanded when the heat of summer came in the following summer. But the Fulton Street Noon-Prayer meetings were different: under Lanphier a season of Noon-Prayer meetings began that continued without interruption until the 1960's.

There is a voluminous literature about the beginning and growth of the Noon-Prayer Meeting movement in New York City and around the world. Within a year there was a 2000-mile prayer chain that included every city and town between Boston and Omaha. More than 1 million people in the U.S. came to Christ during that season of grace, and another million people became believers in the English-speaking nations around the world.

What is not commonly known, however, is that both the 'businessman's lunch' and Lanphier's assignment to do 'systematic visitation' had roots in Thomas Chalmer's vision of societal transformation based on Gospel principles. *If the Noon-Prayer Meetings were the trigger for the New York Revival of 1857-58, then this 19th Century application of Prayer Evangelism principles provided the 'canopy of prayer' that 4000 marketplace leaders had raised during the two years leading up to the famous Fulton Street Prayer Meetings that Lanphier began on September 21, 1857.*

TRANSFORMATION PRINCIPLES IN THE 1857-1858 REVIVAL

More than 25 books have been written about the New York Prayer Revival of 1857-1858, which has inspired countless Christian leaders to establish similar prayer initiatives in their own communities over the last 150 years. Although there has been some mention of the role of 'systematic visitation' in the revival of 1857-1858 by authors such as the Rev. Samuel I. Prime (*The Power of Prayer: The New York Revival of 1858*, pp. 38-39) and Yale historian Timothy L. Smith (*Revivalism & Social Reform*, pp. 65-66), the roots of the 1857-58 prayer meeting in the transformational principles articulated by the Rev. Dr. Thomas Chalmers a generation earlier are not well known.

Recently, however, the present author has obtained a copy of a rare document that outlines how systematic visitation was carried out by the Clinton Avenue Congregational Church in Brooklyn. This document is titled, "Systematic Christian Visitation: Second Annual Report of the Chairman of the Visiting Committee of Clinton Avenue Congregational

Church, Brooklyn, New York. It was published in 1859 by George W. Wood, Printer but has been out of print for the last 150 years.

Not surprisingly, the scriptural basis for the plan of 'systematic visitation' referenced in this document is Luke 10:15—Jesus' instructions concerning house-to-house visitation.

SUMMARY

Today, through Ed Silvoso's books **Prayer Evangelism** and **Transformation** we have well-developed models to reach cities and nations that were only poorly understood in earlier generations. Throughout history, however, the Holy Spirit has spoken to individuals such as John Calvin, Count Zinzendorf, and Thomas Chalmers to become agents of transformation through the power of the Christian Gospel. Today marketplace Christians—like Jeremiah Lanphier in 1857—ask the Lord, "What would you have me to do today?" As we pray this prayer, we anticipate that we will see "greater things" happen in our cities and nations than have occurred in past generations.

We urge you to read and meditate upon the following 19th Century reports on 'Systematic Christian Visitation' and ask the Lord how He wants to use you as an agent of transformation today!

REFERENCES

1. "Christian Visitation," in **The Advocate and Guardian**, volume 23, August 1, 1857, p. 144. Published by the American Female Guardian Society and Home for the Friendless. Provides a concise summary of R. G. Pardee's 1855 "Plan of Systematic Visitation" of households in New York and Brooklyn.

2. "Systematic Visitation, in **The Harvest and the Reapers: Home-Work for All, and How to Do It**, by Harvey Newcomb. Boston: Gould and Lincoln, 1858, pp. 85-92. The author describes systematic visitation as "a plan to carry the Gospel to every creature in the land."

3. **Narratives of Remarkable Conversions and Revival Incidents**, by William C. Conant. New York: Derby & Jackson, 1858, pp.

359-360 and 413. This book includes eyewitness accounts of the "Great Awakening of 1857-58" in New York City, Brooklyn, Newark, and elsewhere.

All three of these publications are currently available in electronic format through Google Books.

Appendix B:

Pray for Newark
Street Adoption Form

ADOPT YOUR STREET

TOGETHER WE CAN
MAKE A DIFFERENCE

To Decrease Crime
Renew Our Schools
Improve Jobs & Housing
Eliminate Poverty
Uproot Corruption
Restore Hope
Transform Our World

Newark's streets are its lifelines. When you adopt a street, you pray blessings over everyone who lives, works, and worships on that street. These prayers will strengthen families, improve neighborhoods, and promote safety and economic development by inviting the Kingdom of God to your street. (Luke 10:1-9)

Changing   Newark's
spiritual   climate—
one street at a time.

www.PrayForNewark.org
www.TransformOurWorld.org

YES,

Sign me up to adopt a Newark street!

☐ I'm willing to pray for the following street:

_____

☐ Name of other Newark street I want to adopt:

_____

MY CONTACT INFORMATION IS:

NAME: _____

EMAIL: _____

PHONE: _____

ADDRESS: _____

CITY: _____

STATE/ZIP: _____

Please fill out this form today or register your street adoption on:
www.PrayForNewark.org

Appendix C:

Additional resources available from transformourworld

The resources listed below are available from Harvest Evangelism through their website: www.transformourworld.org

BOOKS

1. *Transformation: Change the Marketplace and You Change the World*, by Ed Silvoso.
2. *Prayer Evangelism: How to Change the Spiritual Climate Over Your Home, Neighborhood, and City*, by Ed Silvoso.
3. *Anointed for Business: Book and Study Guide*, by Ed Silvoso.
4. *Highways of Holiness: Preparing the Way for the Lord*, by Lloyd Turner.

DVD'S

1. **"Transformation in Newark, New Jersey,"** commissioned by Harvest Evangelism through Media Village
2. **"Transformation in Newark, New Jersey: Part 2, "** Harvest Evangelism/Media Village
3. **"Transformation in the Marketplace,"** Harvest Evangelism/Media Village
4. **"Transformation in Government and Elected Officials,"** Harvest Evangelism/ Media Village
5. **"Transformation in Hawaii,"** Harvest Evangelism/Media Village

These are other resources on Transformation are available in the Resources section of www.transformourworld.org or by calling Harvest Evangelism at 1-800-835-7979.